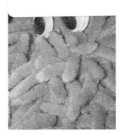

A Modern Classic

by Refried Bean

A Modern Classic

by Refried Bean

for Brian and Anne
Thank you so much,
and thanks again, Mom and Dad

Forward

Well everyone, I have decided to write a little forward to this book. It is my twelfth e-book so far, and I have decided to try to promote them all a little more and sell some soon. I am on a train right now on the way back to New York City from a trip to Greenville, which is my hometown. My apartment that I am going back to is really messy right now and there are a lot of cute little mice hopping around. I need to try to clean it but it is really hard for me to do. Stuff like that has always been hard to do but if I had to climb a tower to type each poem I could because I do have a lot of motivation to write and share ideas.

I have thanked some people in all my books but there are a lot of people I haven't thanked yet. Some of those people are Shannon, Tim, Dr. Nadkarni, Dr. Rojas, Joy, Christina, Ginger, Charles, Judy, Maribeth, three people named Mary, Trilby, and some other friends and teachers who I should eventually try to name. But that is all I am going to say for now. I will try to either add names to the books someday or thank them in other books.

There are also two things that I wanted to share about what I think God has done for me and that I have not written blog posts about yet. One of those things is something I prayed when I was severely depressed as a 23 year old or maybe 24. I cannot describe the emotional pain that I was in perpetually and without hope of ever feeling better. I did not know how I would keep on living for my whole expected life and I asked God if I could cash out my whole reward in heaven and use it on earth to survive. Since then, I have done all kinds of bargaining with all my blessings from all my eternities and sometimes with other people's blessings if I think they don't mind or just have no say in it, and I really think that God might have granted my request because I have had a lot of blessings and relief and help staying alive. And many of those blessings have been friendships, which I think will also last me into heaven. So I am thankful and I have more hope now as I face other mental challenges that erode all kinds of important things in my life and threaten to take away all kinds of security and even things like righteousness.

People who have not turned out to be the community bad person after years of striving to love and serve everyone may not understand what it is like to just not be that great after all, but there is glory in that kind of endurance, too, and I hope that I can encourage people without suggesting that everyone casually spend all their reward all at one time and give up entirely on basic Christian goodness.

I wanted people to know about that, though, because people might wonder how they can wind up with the cheese and chocolate that I have gotten. And on some level, I think it is simply because I prayed, and stayed alive, and because God and people were nice to me.

Anyway, the other thing I wanted to say was that along the way, I became aware of a concept called "The Holy Fool." It is kind of a concept from Orthodox Christianity, and it shows up in literature sometimes, too. And it has to do with people being kind of crazy but being really good and a special blessing to others in a way that just doesn't make sense so much that it does make sense. I read a few stories about people like that, and it can be tempting to force this phenomenon in your life, but as I have strived with all my might to live wisely and take my medicine, I feel that God has given me a dose of foolishness that is really a dream come true. It is, and I wanted to say it as I finish publishing this batch of books, because it is another way that I think God has been faithful and kind. And there might be some question about what I have done on purpose and what just happened. If anyone wants to read more about Holy Fools, Dostoyevsky wrote a book called *The Idiot*, which is about a Holy Fool scenario, and there are a few other examples here and there. Eudora Welty's short story called "A Worn Path," also features a character who is losing many of her important faculties but still exhibits faithfulness and love out of habit. It is inspirational to me, and reminds me of a lady I met in Jamaica when I was in high school. The lady was in an infirmary and was tied to a bench and could not talk, but drew a purple cross on a piece of paper when I sat with her. I thought that was pretty good and I think it is something to strive for even as someone who has a little cursing problem and who sometimes wastes food and can't do basic chores.

These topics probably should have been in a blog post, but I decided to put them in the forward because I think they are things that are behind a lot of my choices and blessings in life, and they are ideas that I wanted to share. Also, I have a little theory that if people imagine themselves being famous and saying stuff in interviews, then they should write those things in their books or on a blog and go ahead and share.

So thanks for reading my writing, everyone, and thanks again to all the people who have been my friends along the way. Hundreds and maybe thousands of people have chronically saved my life, and all these poems and stories and essays are here partially because of them, and so is the miraculous happiness behind many of the jokes.

The Essence of Galore:
More Poems by Refried Bean

Some of my poems are stupid, ain't they?

Until I start saying that people's souls are rabbits

And the scientists discover

That there is some truth to that

and they cut open my brain

And find the lost city of Atlantis

Poem

One of the most glorious things
That Jesus Christ did on earth
Was how he kept it a secret
That our guardian angels
Are friendly little cartoon mice.

Ethical Dilemma

Would you go to church
if you had a condition
that made you compulsively ask God
to burn ten thousand
of people's rewards and blessings in heaven
every time you saw the people?

poem

Is it really fair
to write a poem
about the lizard
on a guy's shoulder
when he is riding a bike?
I mean in a way the poem is already written
and that guy should get credit for it,
or God or the lizard,
but not anyone who thinks of anything to say
when what can be said anyway
except hey, a lizard.

Theology Poem

Guys if I went to seminary my papers would say Jeeeeesus... what a wonderful friend....Jeeeeesus...... what a wonderful friend. How is everyone doing today. Is God constrained by His own character- oh he's not constrained well then does that mean he has to be not constrained? where's the lemonade.

Prognosis

When my illness gets worse
I am going to scream at everyone
and say "Stop hurting the guinea pigs!"
But my guinea pigs will be safe at home
and I will be on the subway
screaming in peoples faces
and telling them
that my guinea pigs did nothing to them
and don't deserve their harassment
and then I will whisper to the people
"can I please have some money,"
and they will give me a hundred dollars
and I will go to a restaurant
and order something that has lemon butter sauce.

Coins

When I get to the mine
the baby dragon will say
all the gold is gone
and we will hike to the shore
and wait for the ships
but a bird will carry a note
that says your reward is gone
so we will go to the city bank
and we will turn the key
but the vault will be empty
and there will be a bug
with a little piece of paper
that says prayer 5555555,
and I will say okay
I do remember that time
in the laundromat on earth
when they played good music
and it was a relief
and I prayed to trade
all my rewards
for their children's futures
and transferred my treasure
to their accounts
and to their peoples
and said they could rummage through it all
and have all my eternities,
so I guess in heaven after seeing
the 45 millionth empty storehouse,
I will just try to get a job at the mall
where I hope they play good music
and maybe I can get a discount
on some clothes that I can wash
in another laundromat
that's clean.

Prediction

My poems stopped making sense
but I didn't care
and just kept writing anyway
until it was pure gibberish
and then just letters,
and then just random marks
that were broken down characters
from another language
that started forming into symbols
and then complex phrases
that were musical notes
that sang themselves
into a song that activated
the secret doorway code
on the great rock of hazmaraz
which did nothing but restart the whole universe
and now here I am
writing this little poem
that I did try my best on
but did kind of just sit here
and say whatever I felt like saying.

poem about The United States

what if they made one person be a new state.
and what if the name of the state
was the person's name like rufus jenkins

Mental Illness

They should make a diagnosis
which is all the disorders combined
and they should call it Super Crazy Deluxe
and if you get diagnosed with that
you should win something.

I should not have touched that lady's food at Starbucks.

My behavior intervention team in heaven
is probably not proud of me
and they are probably scanning their notes
and marking me down on their charts,
and thinking of some way to address the situation,
and they have probably contacted my guardian angels,
which could be sweet little mice,
and asked them to try to steer me near
some people with manners
in hopes that I will learn better,
but what they don't know
is that my guardian angels
like it when I do stuff like that,
and they want me to snatch the food next time,
so there is really a dare on the table
next to the bagel and coffee on the table.

Therapy Journal Therapy

A therapist named Ralphette Ralpherson had been working with a client for five years. This client, named Pedro, had a delusional disorder that made him think that he was a kangaroo who was responsible for telling everyone that they needed to sell cars for a living. He had lost a lot of friends because of the pressure he put on them to get a different job, but a few people did find that the car sales career was just the right path for them. Pedro suffered from depression because of being surrounded every day by people who did things like working at the grocery store or delivering newspapers and who did not tell him that he seemed like a nice kangaroo.

Ralphette, the therapist, was frustrated because she did not see much progress in Pedro's life, and no matter what kind of treatments she used, or what kinds of logic she presented, Pedro always still thought that he was a kangaroo car sales recruiter. Ralphette decided to write about the situation and presented the case in a Psychology journal that was dedicated to describing psychiatric conditions that seemed impossible to treat.

One day soon after it was published, Pedro came into her office and said, "Ralphette, I have something to tell you. All this time I have thought that I was a kangaroo who was supposed to convince everyone to sell cars. But the other day I was at a college library trying to persuade all the biology majors to quit their major, and when I was there I found a psychology journal and read it. And there was this article about someone just like me, and I realized that I am not a kangaroo!"

Ralphette did not know what to say. She was not able to tell if Pedro realized that the article was specifically about him. "Pedro," she said, "I am so glad that you have had this breakthrough!"

"Me too," said Pedro. "I wish everyone could get cured like me, and I might try to start helping everyone become a therapist like you. I will always remember this, kind of like an elephant. In fact I think I might be an elephant.

Backpack Story

Ralph Ralpherson usually carried a backpack everywhere he went. One day, he decided not to take it with him to go buy a coffee at the coffee shop. The lightness that he felt from not having the backpack made him almost feel like he could fly. It gave him a feeling of freedom, and he sensed less responsibility to get important things done. He ordered a bigger coffee than usual, and got whipped cream with sprinkles. Later, he skipped home singing a song.

The next day, he decided to leave the backpack home again, and he again felt a sense of freedom that soon escalated into a feeling of complete punk rebellion. He knocked over garbage cans as he walked, and threw litter on the ground. For his finale, he grabbed someone's unattended bookbag on the way out of the coffee shop after ordering a triple mocha milkshake. On his way home, the weight of the stolen bookbag started to drag him back into reality, and he realized that his behavior did not match the way he really wanted to live. He took a risk and went all the way to his apartment, put on his own bookbag, and took the bookbag he stole back to the coffee shop.

When he got there, he turned it in and apologized. The lady whose backpack it was listened to his story and said, "Wow, that is crazy. I guess it is good for you to carry your backpack more often. And now I know to be more careful with mine. I think I will give you a reward."

The lady reached into her backpack and pulled out some heavy rolls of quarters. "I think I will give you these quarters. They will make your backpack heavier so you won't be as tempted to fling it off and run around doing crazy stuff."

"Thank you so much," said Ralph. "I was worried that I would spray paint grafitti everywhere, but now I can keep doing what I am supposed to. And I might use some of the quarters for laundry, because it has kind of piled up."

"I was hoping so," said the nice backpack person. "Because I work at the laundromat and I like quarters and I like people who don't spray paint my building."

Ralph and the nice backpack person, whose name was Ralphette, got married and helped each other carry heavy loads of laundry every day.

Shattered

If you look in the mirror
and your reflection is cracked,
is it because the mirror is broken,
or because you're broken?

poem

What if there was a multiple choice test
with one question that had a thousand choices
and only one of those choices was the right answer?

poem

When I donate my brain to science
they are probably going to find
my lost set of keys in the middle of it.

Poem

What if you were in the hospital
And it was the Neurology Unit
And they gave you some Jello
And it was gray and wrinkled.

Some Concept

I do not have God wrapped around my little finger.
He does not have to do everything I say or even anything.
I don't ask him to go down to the corner and fetch me some
salvation.
I don't have him get right on it when I have a chore to do myself.
Do you know who cleans the cages of my pet guinea pigs?
I do it myself but the Holy Spirit does probably help me a little bit.
And God does make the cages exist perpetually
without even a blink that I am aware of although for all we know
the world could be ceasing to exist
for tiny miliseconds that we do not know about.
But if God could do that
then couldn't he also provide me with some extra cash?
That is why I go ahead and pray some prayers,
and try to pray those prayers
when I am standing next to someone
who seems like a good person
so God might think that's who prayed.

God Cannot Be Mocked.

Do not be deceived.
God cannot be mocked.
But it is okay to shimmy down the street
going Walla walla walla ding dang ding ding dang ding dang.
Why would God be mad about that.
I mean you did nothing rude except have a good time.
Watch. I will say it now. Walla walla walla okay I am scared.

poem

What if you were with some people
and you thought you had nothing in common
but it turns out that you all had eaten
a peanut butter milkshake
on the exact same day
at the exact same time in 1985.
And then when you realized that
you also realized that you all had great great relatives
who went to the zoo on the same day
a hundred years before you were born.
People say well how would you know.
Well it would be because all of you carried
an old ticket around to remind you
to be nice to people
who you have nothing in common with.

Stat

I think I am going to call 911
and tell them
that one in three or four children
have been abused.

A Modern Classic

What if you tried to text a friend
to ask about something
and spellcheck turned your message
into a novel and it became a modern classic.

Casino Poem

The angel animals
in heaven
who are perpetually gambling
on our behalf
with each gold coin
that they are given
when we say and do the right thing
might win big
with the dollar they get
when people say
they don't believe
in gambling angel mice.

Math Poem

I think that eleven people should get together
and each try to guess the last number of Pi,
and the eleventh person can guess
that there is no last number,
and one of them has to be right,
so then they could get a special Math Prize for it
and share it among themselves.

**On a Scale of Oppression, Persecution,
Torture, Crucifixion,
Crushed for our Transgressions**

People should be careful
saying that not getting ice cream
is persecution.
They should also be careful
saying that it is not.

Walla Walla Ding Dang

If I had been a missionary,
I could have written letters
to all the people I really loved
and said, "Would you please pray with me
for the children of Walla Walla Ding Dang?"
but I am not a missionary,
so all I can do is pray for the children
of Walla Walla Ding Dang myself,
and wish I could be there to see their faces
when they wake up on Christmas morning
and see all the Bing Bang Challa challa hoop doop
walla walla shuffle bop bring brang loop de loop
roople doops that I asked God to give them.

Social Work Placement

When y'all were an intern
did you hear the janitor tell someone
that you weren't that good of an intern?
Well that is what happened to me.
But I am not sad and mad.
I think it is funny.
So the janitor
does not need to mop up my tears.
The janitor will have to use
the cleaning solution
that I hid.

Rules and Regulations

When I call senators
I do not tell them
that I had ancestors in the revolution.
I do not say "Great job fellas."
I do not call them commies to their face.
And I do not tell them my personal problems
unless it is because of a bill that they passed.
I do not ask them to wave at me on C-Span.
I do not ask them to write the words "Happy Birthday"
in one of their bills.
I do not pretend to be a dignitary from another country
or a prank caller pretending to be a dignitary
or a prank caller pretending to be a different prank caller.
I just give the senators a few helpful hints and suggestions,
and tell them how I think they should vote,
in case they need someone to blame it on
when the bill gets messed up
because no one ever said
"Great job fellas,"
or surprised everyone
with a fun round of Bingo
when the guards weren't looking.

Some people.

Some people are good but wrong.
Some people are right but bad.
Some people are bad and wrong
but are telling the truth.
Some people are good and right
and are telling the truth
but they are being mean.
Some people are nice
but aren't telling the truth.
Some people are nice and right
and good and are telling the truth
but aren't doing what they are supposed to.
Some people are bad and wrong
and mean and aren't telling the truth
and aren't doing what they are supposed to.
Some people are mad.

Cool Aid

I am going to start a new cult
And see if Jesus Christ wants to join.
It will be for people who rise from the dead
and forgive people for their sins.
I will say do you want to accept yourself
As my personal lord and savior.
Jesus will say of course.
And I will say well at our meetings
We need some people to bring snacks.

asking therapist if therapist is mad at me

Therapist says
no I have never been mad at you

I say that is great
but are you not mad
because you are
suppressing your anger

Therapist says no
I have no anger to suppress.

I say good I am relieved
but is that because
you have trained yourself
not to have anger
about things that
you should be angry about.

Therapist says no
I really can't think
of any reason to be mad.

I say is that because
you are blinded by anger.

This might be when
therapist starts to get a little mad.

**Shame shame shame
I know your name.**

What people really need
Instead of recognition
Is acceptance.
But sometimes true acceptance
Is in the form of recognition.
And isn't recognition
Love?

Recipe for trouble

Carving out a life
means there will probably be scraps
And maybe one of my scraps
Is when I walk down the street
Calling people names.
If life is gingerbread
Then I can reuse those scraps somehow,
Maybe in a poem about how I hope
That I don't get caught.

You can't fool God all the time
But you can fool him never of the time.

If I see a person
helping another person
who is suffering,
I give them each
a piece of pizza
in hopes that
it will mean
that I can get
some of their reward
in heaven.

How Rude

Well excuuuuuse me.
From jury duty.

Mystery Idea

What if you were on a jury for a murder case
and then you figured out
that the defendant was innocent
and the person who really did it
was on the jury with you.

A Shocking Revelation

Fifi arrived at the courthouse an entire hour before jury selection but had a coffee to drink and a phone to read the news on. She sat on the benches outside the courtroom and watched other possible jury members show up and was excited as the process got going. She was even more excited when she was chosen, because she had never served on a jury before. Usually when they called her name at each court summons, she reminded them that she had mental illness, and they either excused her or just didn't select her. But she had been feeling better for several years after joining a creative writing group and keeping a part time job at the grocery store that gave her a lot of free food, so this time she kept quiet and got selected.

"Hi, everyone," she said to the other eleven jurors when they introduced themselves in the conference room that looked like it was from a TV show. "I think I might be able to get us some free donuts every single day."

"That's great," said a young athletic looking guy who wore a giant neon wristwatch and had agreed to keep track of time for everyone.

"I'll take three chocolate, one jelly, and a powdered-- not stale," said the largest jury member.

Most of the jury members laughed a little while and introduced themselves to each other. The jury cop joined in, too, but told everyone not to be too good at being jury members or they would make them the jury every time.

Fifi was enjoying being on the jury but got nervous when it turned out to be a murder case. It was a case where a janitor was being blamed for the death of a sales executive who had been working late one night in one of the tall buildings near the court building. He had been killed with an electric jolt from a joke pen that shocked people. It wasn't supposed to be able to hurt anyone, but someone had rigged it to give a hundred times the shock. The janitor was taking wiring and engineering classes on weekends and was the only one who was clocked in at work that night, so he was charged with the crime almost immediately.

Fifi started having doubts about whether she could handle the case, but she knew that it was too late to turn back now. She decided to call an emotional support hotline each night and just tell them her feelings without sharing details of the case. Several days passed, and she still felt a little bit depressed and anxious as the court case progressed and the jury learned more about what happened.

"I did not hurt anyone," said the janitor in court. I have never done violence in my life. I would never get a gag pen like that. I do not think it is funny to shock people. I do not even tell anyone anything surprising."

After the janitor testified, the jury members talked about the case with each other. One of the guys who took most of the notes got mad when the jury started to agree that the janitor could not have done it.

"Of course he did it," the note taker said, putting his pen down. "He was the only one who knew about the extra exit through the back janitor closet. Anyone else would have used their pass key and had the stripe reader marked. "See?" The notetaker reached in his shirt pocket and grabbed a mess of cards and a couple of other pens that were metal and heavy. He then held out a red and white plastic card with a magnetic stripe and three holes in it. It said "Companybrand," which was the name of the agency that the janitor and the victim had worked for.

"Where did you get that?" said the largest juror.

The notetaker's face got red, as if he had realized he made a mistake.

People figured out quickly that the notetaker was a bad guy and they started to panic. The jury cop stepped forward to see what was going on, and the athletic guy with the neon watch reached for the extra pens on the table with lightning speed. But the notetaker knocked them away from him and started to try to grab his throat. Fifi acted fast and picked up a pen, jammed it into the notetakers arm, and pressed the metal button on top. It shocked them both with a force that knocked the notetaker to the ground and stunned Fifi. The jury cop then quickly arrested the notetaker, who was still alive, and they called an ambulance.

"I think we have our real murderer," said the largest jury guy.

It was true. The note taker was a rival businessman who was trying to get a promotion from the company as well as advance his secret stock in the competitor's business. He had snuck in the building, committed the crime, and framed the janitor. Then, just to be safe, he hacked the jury system and arranged to be a juror for the trial. But that was where he had overdone it.

Fifi ate some donuts and juice as she sat in a chair trying to recover from being shocked, and she was even more shocked that she had just been through something like that. When the paramedics got there, she decided to check into a hospital just to be safe. They kept her there for several days, but she felt mostly okay almost immediately. In fact, she felt great, and her depression was almost completely gone after that. Some of her friends thought it could be from the feelings of being a hero, but she always said that it must have been from the free electric shock treatment.

Hmm I wonder how I figured this out

If you are a cashier
and you are mad at people
then instead of saying
"Have a great day,"
You could say
"Have a gray day,"
and people would probably not know.

A lunch break for the jury

I am going to sue myself
for all my mistakes,
and the judge,
who is me,
and the jury,
who is me,
and the people watching,
who is me,
will find myself guilty,
and order
that I order
a cheeseburger
and a coke,
and call it even,
and call it a day,
but not A Great Day
of Judgement.

Good Enough For Me

When I die,
people will not say,
"Surely that was the Messiah."
At this point,
I might not even be able to pass
a basic criminal background check.
But I know that there are some people
still walking among us
who can say
when questioned
that when they were with me
the usual demons
were no longer able
to feast upon their flesh.

Money is for this sometimes

I just discovered some wonderful candy-themed hot wheels toys online but I have peeps stuffed animals and I can eat Mike and Ike's and I do not need to spend 110 dollars on something that yeah I will probably go ahead and order okay thanks everyone.

Totinos One dollar Pizzas.

I do not know what will happen
on Judgement Day
when there is a reckoning,
but it could be as simple
as some kind of roll call,
and God tells me in front of everyone
that in my life
I ate the equivalent
of ten grocery stores.
And then maybe everyone will say Wow!
And then God will say
So I am putting you in a community
with a lot of grocery stores.
And I will say thank you so much.
And God will say
you already said thank you a lot.
And I will say yeah
because I like frozen pizza and Coke.
And then there will be thunder
and it will be someone else's turn,
and they like Unicorns, rainbows,
caramel pudding with vanilla cake,
and skyship food tour ventures
for everyone in sight.

20 sufferings and a lot of chocolate.

No need to list out everything.
But there have been some snickers.

The Way It Is

I think that a strategy
to make sure
all your prayers get answered
is to pray for everything to be
exactly the way it is.

Request

What if you were suffering
and people said
"How can I pray for you?"
And you said,
"I just want a party castle
someday in heaven."

Loopdeeloop

I shouldn't get credit for what is really Schizophrenia.
And the Schizophrenia should not get credit for the Aspergers.
And Aspergers should not get credit for the Christianity.
And Christianity should not get credit for God's mercy.
And God's mercy should not get credit for God himself.
But God himself should get credit for me.

proudly planting a flag at sea level

the heights of the heroes and depths of the foes
the chasm of sin and the good no one knows.

when people are terrible they can be great
and just being normal is like a clean slate.

and everyone better can climb up so high
but just breaking even took such a great try.

so while there is glory way far up above,
in low humble places there's peace, hope, and love.

The dawning light of maple glaze

They could have called cake "sugar bread"
couldn't they have?
And Dominoes "dot game shuffle."
But some things we will never know
and when I get to heaven
I am hoping to be grouped with some other people
who have wasted some bacon and sausage sometimes
and do feel bad about it
but don't think it is the worst thing that can be done
or at least don't know that it is the worst.
Get it? Worst? Wurst?
Where am I going with this discussion?
Some things we will never know.

Kindling

No one likes me,
and there is nothing for me in this life
Except coffee with a lot of cream and sugar,
So I stay alive for that
And for the remote possibility
that I might qualify
For the adequate common decency award
given out on Judgement Day
for all the people who really just wanted friends.
But after all of the award losers
walk the long aisle through all of humanity to get our certificates,
We will gradually find our way to the campfires,
Where we will burn our mean papers,
and maybe someone will have also brought marshmallows.

Poem

Abuse victims will not appreciate this
But that lobster sandwich did rape me didn't it.
It tasted like celery and I don't like celery.
I looked forward to it for two days
and now it has ruined my vacation.
They do it on purpose so you will buy something else.
And I did buy a Coke and a Twix.
And I do have a nice life except for that lobster sandwich
and some other bad things that have happened.
And some people are like yeah we are mad.
They are saying ok we gave you a chance
to not offend us by comparing eating lobster
to one of the worst things that can happen to someone.
Well I gave that lobster sandwich a chance to be yummy didn't I.

But it made its choice to be in this poem
and to not just hurt me but hurt all of the people
who are now involved in this legal case
and who now have to miss their own birthday party to be at my trial.
That includes anyone who knows about this poem.

Now people are really mad.
But would they be so mad
if they knew that the trial was being catered
by a gourmet food company?
Hmm what should be on the menu?
Are some people saying maybe not that lobster?
Well I guess we have our verdict don't we.
People are saying the verdict is that my poem tastes like celery.
Well how dare you.
How dare you compare my poem
to one of the worst things that can happen to someone.

poem

I feel humbled by everyone's support,
like reminded that I am from dust,
and one of God's little creatures,
and just a person doing what is expected,
but am I really being humble?
or is it more like I am just lazy and dirty?

poem

I am interested in starting a program
called Operation How are you.
where the main point is to
say "how are you" to people.
And really I have already said that lots of times
 so I guess it is all a big success.

poem

If people are on a plane
 that is taking off
and they feel scared
I just tell them
to close their eyes
and pretend that they are safe.

Ethical dilemma

If you are in a cab going to the food pantry and you see a parked car with keys stuck in the trunk, do you stop and try to find the owner or just hope for the best? It's honestly not that easy to figure out in real life. But if you have to have the challenge of an ethical dilemma, why shouldn't someone else have the challenge of not being able to find their keys. Therein lies the answer, or might I say the key to understanding, which might be a key that you accidentally left in the van's trunk of your mind and a lot of people have known you and wanted to say something but were on their way to the food pantry.

poem

If you ever don't know someone's name,
do you just call them Jamilope?
I don't, because that is probably not their name.

Idea

You know what I think a good defense
would be to keep a city safe?
I think it would be smart to design all the buildings
in a way that makes them all look
like they have already been destroyed,
like making the whole city
look like it is a pile of rubble
so no one tries to attack it.

Namescake

If you sold caramel cake
and your name was Caroline,
don't you think it would be smart
to change your name
to Carameline?

Poem

Fall is like
the woods
burning
ain't it.

The Origin of Bingo

One time, in a hospital for people who had been injured in highly competitive sports games, a recreational therapist arranged for a bingo session with snacks. Everyone had such a good time choosing their cards and eating candy and soft drinks and listening to the therapist call out bingo numbers. Something different about this game is that everyone tried to let everyone else win, and they would keep some of their spaces uncovered even after the numbers had been called. For every game, the therapist would finish calling out the bingo numbers and there would still be no winner. Everyone would say, "I guess it is a tie," and they would raise their cups of soda in a toast. The bingo group decided to play bingo for many years, and they loved each other so much that even after everyone was in heaven, they played Bingo there, too, and no one would ever try to win. In fact, no one ever actually won a game of bingo, and they played for 45 million eternities, until the love was so fierce that the Bingo chips started glowing. Eventually, the Bingo chips exploded into stars, which exploded again, and created some of the elements now used in plastic Bingo chips. In fact, that is how the game of Bingo originated.

Cooking Safety

I didn't have any clean knives
to kill myself with
even though just hours earlier
I had washed several butcher knives
at the volunteer project
where we tried to help children cook.
They cut up vegetables,
and just cut up,
and cut up my peace of mind permanently
by lunging at each other with sharp blades.
My shredded optimism
was the secret ingredient of the chili,
which I think would have tasted better
with a nice cool glob of sour cream.

Sideline

Everyone's welcome at the marathon
although in the end
I don't really think people
want me there
with my poster
that says
Y'all think you are so great.

Adoption Poem

You know how people adopt kids
well what if people can adopt
other kinds of family
like moms or maybe
people can adopt people
as inanimate objects
like refrigerators or radios.

Book Return

If I owned a public library
I think a good way to make extra money
would be to make the trash can
the book return place
so all the books get lost
and people pay huge fines.

The Path of The Rolling Night Fire

Some people
are sounding the war gong
But I am here to say
That Chiquita
Like Chiquita bananas
should have a clothing line.
And the soldier mice will say
"You will suffer me,"
Just like in the movies,
But one little mouse will say
"I want my mommy,"
So they will make him a cook.
And we all know what you will do.
You will say
"I forgot my wallet,"
And then who will pay.
Well it will be Jesus Christ
With his blood on the cross.

A Christmas Poem

The evil beasts
are feasting on our heartbreak
and our sorrow
is like slop in their troughs
until they choke
on Christ in the manger.

Servants of the Most Low

In the Bible it says stuff
about multiple heavens
and I still don't understand earth
but what if some heavens
like maybe the fifth heaven
or second heaven
are below some of the hells
so that the smell of peppermint
and gingerbread and oranges
wafts up to the next level
and makes those people
not know how to escape.

Theology from the Mine

I told my atheist friend
about predestination
where God's intervention
is irresistible
and my friend said
"So I am damned to heaven?"

Breaks

If you work in a busy retail store
with people asking you questions all the time,
It is good to split your fifteen minute break
into fifteen one minute breaks,
so if someone bothers you,
you can stop them midsentence
and say "Sorry, but I am taking a one minute break."
And then walk off.

cursive and red ink

God is not pleased
With some of my ways and means.
And sayings and doings
And glances and musings.
With some of my wheelings and dealings
And thoughts and feelings.
And my no good two faced underhanded
yellow bellied crooked swindles.
My snap flap clap trap escpades.
And yet my name is written
In the one and only
Book of life
And the ink and signature
Was probably lifted
With a carbon print
Right off of one of my traffic tickets.

What is confusing

praying for each person
To be so blessed
And so loved
That everyone turns on them
And says hey that's not fair
And then takes their
prize lunch box.

Salvation is not all that God does

When people repay my kindness
With ding dang ding dang
Chopple chopple bing bang
I stand up and sing a song of freedom
And I open a briefcase
With a little mouse inside
That holds a tiny poster saying
Everything God does
Is salvation.

There is no frigate like a frigate

I want to say
Service is power
And fentanyl is murder

But some want to say
Capitalism is slavery
And jail is torture

So I will have to say
That words are words
and meaning is meaning

And though the dictionary
Isn't the only book
It can get people pretty far

**If you don't do your laundry
You can't be the magic roofaloo.**

But if the laundromat burns

Then what do you do

A who and a blue and a doodle-ee do.

Why do chores when you want to have fun

If you give me five dollars then this poem is done.

Elephant Poem

If people call you elephantine,
just remember that the elephants
have also been called elephantine.

poem

What if whenever
you met people's dogs
you did what dogs do
and sniffed the dog's butts.

poem

What if they made a Catholic church
that was for former Protestants
and it was called
Our Lady of Renunciation.

Poem

Do you ever laugh so hard
That you fear for your safety?
I don't.
I rarely laugh at all
And sometimes
my nose itches on the inside.

Poem

In the end
All the good people will say
That all the bad people
Played right into our hand.

Cheese shop Poem

When people are working
at the cheese shop
Do you think that really
They might just be showing off
That they work in a cheese shop

Poem

If your heart is broken
Because your computer is broken
Does it mean your heart is a computer?
No.
Your heart is just a bloody soft tissue organ
Like what monsters hold up in their hand
In the movies you used to watch on your computer

Theology test

If you put your name
On the paper
Then you will get
Partial credit
For everything
You've ever done
And full credit
For all the answers
Of the one valedictorian
From all the schools
that tell the truth.

Poem

I wonder if there is such thing
As demon possessed demons.

Well what if some prayers are cheesy

guys
would y'all say
that my prayers for new york
 have gotten a little stale.
i think you are right.
i mean it has gotten to the point
where I just ask God
to give everyone
three hundred dollars in their pocket each day.
and i think people want a little more out of life
or just don't want me to get credit
for the cash
even though I used all my credit
from sitting on the train
asking God for cash
to ask for more cash
but that doesn't mean
it is because of me
that people are wearing shoes
and because of me
that there are buildings,
but we don't know what isn't
because of me either,
because what if some day
I ask God to go back in time
and provide a lot of pizza
for a lot of people,
and how do we know
that is not how New York
got started.

An Ad for Philadelphia

those people at the philadelphia train station
were just darling werent they
i mean i wish they were all my coworkers in an office.
In fact I would like to start a little ad agency
called the philadelphia train station agency
so we can all work for the same company.
and we can all spray paint over all the ads at the train station
and then play cards.
Well people say I they dont think that is really an ad agency.
Well what do you know about ad agencies
if you haven't even been
to the philadelphia train station.

No Joke

People might say
that some of my jokes are blasphemous
but it might be more blasphemous
to not ever risk blasphemy
for a good cause.

Rule

You know what they say:
You're only as good
as your fourth poem
that you wrote
fifteen years ago.

Just Saying

Some people
have worked very hard
for what they have
but some people
have worked very hard
for what they don't have.

Every now and then

The people in the history classes of tomorrow
Are laughing at us right now
And saying what a bunch of morons
But what do they know
They're from a time
When things were easier

Things I don't understand

When people push you into the mud
and then call you muddy

When people pay the kidnappers the ransom
After you're already dead

A poem I found in my mind

When people are sad because they lose something
Sometimes everyone says
"You should be thankful for what you have"
But if you are sad about losing something
then isn't that proof that you were really thankful for it?

The Christmas Lemon

A long time ago, in a remote suburban household, there lived a sweet little lemon and his family, which was mostly limes. They were eating dinner one night during the holidays and the lemon said, "It seems like cranberries are getting all the attention at Christmas time and Thanksgiving. People keep eating cranberry sauce and eating cranberry scones. It really hurts my feelings.

The lemon's dad, who was a lime, said, "Well we should all just be thankful for what we have, but maybe you should write a letter to Santa Claus and ask him about it." The lemon did that, and Santa sent him a letter that said, "That is not really my problem. You need to contact Jesus Christ about it. Santa wrote the phone number of Jesus Christ on the letter, and the lemon called him as soon as he could.

When the lemon called Jesus Christ, Jesus could not answer because he was celebrating Chanukah with his family. But on the fifth or sixth day, Jesus called the lemon and asked him what was going on.

"It seems like cranberries are getting all the attention," said the lemon.

"Yes, I am aware of that situation," said Jesus. "But some people do use a lemon sauce with gingerbread." You just mix lemon juice with butter and sugar, and maybe water and cornstarch.

"Ok, thank you so much, Jesus."

"You're welcome. Talking to you gives me the idea to serve lemon lime punch at the Christmas party this year in heaven, so thanks for contacting me.

The lemon said goodbye and had a happy and relieved feeling in his mind. He told his family about it and they were very excited to think about all the people in heaven drinking lemon lime punch at the Christmas party.

And everyone especially was happy on Christmas morning, when the lemons and limes woke up and found that there was a new Nintendo game system left there by Jesus Christ.

poem

People can think what they want
but they would probably be schizophrenic too
if they lived in New York City.

Confession

I do want to be famous
so that some day
the encyclopedias will say
"In later years,
she retreated into a fantasy world
of imaginary cartoon mice."

The Fruit of Repentance:
More Blog Posts by Refried Bean

Coldline

Well everyone I had a psychological problem that wasn't that bad but kind of bad and I tried to call a hotline just to feel better but they said they had an emergency call come in and ended my call. Well I do not know why except maybe I sounded too chipper and not enough like I was about to throw myself into a wood chipper.

Some lines about the DMV

Well everyone, I went to the DMV today, and honestly it wasn't a bad experience. I was getting a drivers license after a time of not driving for a while. I had to wait for an hour and then another hour, and they call out people's numbers the whole time. Like there is a screen with a lot of numbers. I actually think they should consider combining it with some kind of Bingo game, and if you win, then you don't have to wait as long. I mean they could almost do that as it is, like choose a few numbers to call immediately for no reason but to make those people winners who don't have to wait in line. And then after that they could just start passing out cash. That is kind of what they did today except it was me paying the 66 dollars.

Out of the loop

This is random but I for a long time have thought that the Massachusetts Institute of Technology was in Texas. I wonder if I applied there and told them that then they might think that it is so stupid it actually must be something past being smart you know like so high up intelligence scales that it actually is a certain kind of stupid that is off the charts, or maybe if intelligence loops around then that is the reason for my thinking. But I do not want to go there so I think that if I applied then that would also be because of the loop.

Fast feast

This might be something I should just post on facebook but I am feeling shy so I am writing it on my blog. There is a scene in Lord of the Rings with this bad steward fake king guy and he has a feast of food laid out in front of him and one of the hobbits is his servant and the hobbit sings a song and there is slow motion video of the king eating the food like a pig and he is gnawing at the meat and tomato juice runs down his face and it is supposed to be related to how much of a bad person he is. I think of him sometimes when I eat something like wings, really probably every time I eat wings, and during my depressions a long time ago I would sometimes feel like I was just like him when I would eat hungrily or do something like drink a whole pitcher of kool aid, which I did sometimes because life was hard.

Anyway I just got home from walking to go get food and I turned on the Return of the King movie on my computer, which I haven't watched for a while, and right as it was starting, it was that scene, and it is funny because I just got wings. So that is pretty hilarious because basically now it will be like a mirror of me eating my food but I am not going to let it get me down everyone. But really honestly it was kind of greedy for me to go get the food I got because I just had good food yesterday. But it doesn't mean that I am a bad steward or king or that I should be burnt alive like what happens to him towards the end of the movie. And if that scene is just like me, maybe there are other scenes from other movies that are also me, and maybe one of those movies is the Care Bears movie, and I should remember that I also eat Reese's pieces sometimes, kind of like E.T.

A Guessing game with no hints

Well everyone, I found a great new doctor today and hopefully I can keep being her patient, because she helped me a lot. I feel that she did not mind me explaining my condition in euphemisms because of the way I am so embarrassed by health problems and terms, and when I said stuff like "such and such if you know what I mean but I don't want to say," she knew just what to prescribe. Probably after a few visits I can just show up and look away in shame and she will know exactly what the diagnosis is. I think that really that is what great health care is all about, and an unlabeled grab bag system at the drug store might work out well for everyone too.

Confidential

This blog post is about something confidential because I signed a form saying that I would not share any information about it. I'll give you a hint though. The hint is that I can't tell you anything about it.

Using my best Judgement

Well everyone, Tuesday I have to report for jury duty. I think that I should go with a verdict already decided just to save time. This might make them pick me, too, when they are choosing the jury members. If they say, okay, the next juror we are considering, what is your name, etc. And I will say my name is Refried Bean and I find the defendant not guilty.

The fruit flies are not paying their share of the rent

Well everyone, how are you doing. I am doing great. I have been cleaning my apartment a little bit this week and got a free shelf that I am very thankful for. I have thrown out about thirteen bags of trash which was a worse situation than I thought. But I really think that a clean apartment is right around the corner. And I am talking about my apartment like in a few days- not about other apartments that are literally around the corner.

Crimony

Well everyone, I haven't written that much on this blog lately, but that is because I got a little shaken up by a background check for volunteering. For a while, it seemed like I was going to fail the criminal background check when I haven't committed any crimes, and I freaked out. I just freaked out and started running around town committing crimes in a panic, so now I will probably fail all future criminal background checks. Just joking. But the process was really traumatizing and I don't know if I will still be able to do the kind of volunteering I was trying to do. It did turn out that the background check went through okay and I am either not dangerous or am just being closely monitored and the clearance is just a decoy to make me walk past police stations in an overconfident way until suddenly I absent-mindedly walk in the exit door of the subway instead of the turnstile and I am no longer allowed to do anything but crimes.

Not a game

Well everyone, today is September 22. I just got back from a trip to SC. It was really fun and I got to stay in a hotel, which I almost never get to do. I went to my old college for a reunion of all the mascots from over the years. But of course not all the mascots could be there, and I missed the final field ceremony, which would have been great. I went to the game but got delayed and went in the wrong gate and could not tolerate the crowd, and I felt like the conspiracy was torturing me and I left while I still could without getting trapped where a cab could not reach me. Later I thought maybe I should have tried harder to stay but I just couldn't. So sometimes I have a sad feeling, but mostly I am glad I went. It brought back a lot of memories of mascot days, but it also made me feel a little traumatized. I could barely watch the new mascots entertain everyone.

Now I am back home with my wonderful pet guinea pigs who are all three together in the same cage and getting along great. So everything is great except for all the headlines that suggest we are on the brink of nuclear war with countries that we could have bombed with regular bombs at any time in the last twenty years. And people are also about to take away health care and try that same pre-existing condition scam that was also a problem for twenty years and should never have been tolerated.

So I am thinking about heaven sometimes and how things will be different and I will mostly be playing cards in the basement of some stone building in a green valley with a lot of slushie delivery services nearby. Fred, Roger, and Dave, who are my guinea pigs, will no longer need a cage and will probably also be playing cards with me and my friends, and we will all have a little stash of gold coins and other interesting valuables on the table. And I will get dealt five jokers and win a golden pocket watch that projects a portal to any one of the billions of USC games being played throughout eternity.

This post should be in a library

Well hi everyone, I am typing this at the library. You guys did not know that I knew where a library was did you. Well I am at the library now so now who has the last laugh. Well it isn't me because we are supposed to be quiet at the library. I am waiting here for my support group that starts at 6:15. There was a jigsaw puzzle downstairs when I got here and the picture was just of the garage of a normal house. I think that is pretty funny because it is kind of like an art movement of hyper realism or just realism except it is so normal that being an image for a jigsaw puzzle is abnormal which then makes it interesting again.

The reason I am going to the support group is because I think that people probably picked that puzzle out just to entertain me and have also tampered with every single aspect of every day life and influenced every single interaction I have with anyone I talk to or don't talk to. Even though I think everyone is in on it, it still seems wrong and weird to confront people about it every time something bothers me, so I go to this group where I can say okay the conspiracy is bothering me.

Anyway I ate at IHOP earlier so now who's laughing. Well it still isn't me because I am at the library just like I was a few minutes ago when I started this post, and just like I was a few seconds ago when I said "just like a few minutes ago when I started this post."

Copyright statement

Today I thought of a defense if I ever have copyright problems in any of my books, which is to say that I am a conscientious objector for copyright law. I mean who can argue with that? I do worry about things like brand names not wanting free advertising, or not being allowed to freely share a facebook share, or worst of all, accidentally copying entire books by other people because of a mix of photographic memory and dementia. I mean of course I am joking, but I do have weird mental gifts and deficits, and occasional feelings of false deja vu when I write, and I have permanently deleted about twenty poems because of these kinds of fears. And I can't just go back and reread every book I have ever read to be safe each time I write a poem. And people say no, you know when you copy someone and you know that you have been a very bad person who pretended that you wrote *Les Miserables* and *Tale of Two Cities*. But actually, that is not true, and I am still only at the level where I pretend that I have *read* the classics, not written them. I really don't always know which Amtrak stations all my trains of thoughts departed from, and even if I did, I would still probably get it mixed up with the train station in the new novel I am working on called *Anna Karenina*.

Happy Belated Halloween

Well everyone, how are you doing. Today is November 11. It is one of my favorite days. Because it is 11/11. And I do remember when it was 11:11 on 11/11/11. I think I was at Barnes and Noble on that day. That is where I used to work.

I have not posted in a while because the internet is not working at my apartment. Also I have been doing a lot of volunteer work. It is sad to not have done many blog posts, because I did have a lot to write about last month. One of the things I might have written about was how I went to a Halloween party at the Natural History Museum. I was a shark for Halloween and my costume was kind of one of those ridiculous costumes that is like a whole big costume like Eddie Murphy on Saturday Night Live. I feel like the shark costume also had another effect of implying that I was immersed in water, since sharks have to swim in water to live, and I think that this made the natural history museum also have a Halloween costume by pretending to be an aquarium for Halloween. Or it could be seen like a flood in the fossil museum that represents billions of years, so it is like an evolution museum dressing up as a Creation museum for Halloween. Is that weird to think that way? That is how I interpret things sometimes.

Anyway, I also gave out a lot of candy for Halloween. I gave out about forty bags of candy and it went well, but I regretted not including Tootsie Pops, which is something I considered giving out and then didn't. And then after Halloween I got a huge bag of Tootsie Pops to kind of make up for it but now I have almost 80 Tootsie Pops and Halloween is over. So that is a little confusing, But anyway I think I have figured out that Tootsie Pops or Blow Pops or Caramel Apple Pops can make the difference in seeming like you are handing out whole handfuls of candy on Halloween. Like you can do two snack size candies like Nerds or Skittles or M and Ms, and then if you simply add a good lollipop then all of a sudden it is like a wad of candy that seems like some kind of variety assortment. Every year I learn something new like that. Do y'all remember when I gave out Mexican gum for Halloween? And I gave out Now and Laters, which are rare, and I did not do well and had too much left over and then the next day some of the candy I passed out was on an internet list of candy that people supposedly don't like.

I just thought of an idea for a candy which is what if there was a lollipop shaped exactly like the inside of your mouth. Kind of like a candy retainer. In fact that could be the name of the candy is "Candy Retainers," and it is a giant mouth shaped candy that lasts for hours.

Happy Thanksgiving, Everyone!

Well everyone, how are you doing. I am at Whole Foods right now and hopefully Amazon and Whole Foods have taken over everyone's lives and my life so much that they have a savings fund for me and have already ordered some Christmas presents that I will find at my apartment when I get home. I am hoping for some Hot Wheels cars and some orange Hot Wheels tracks to make wall shelves out of.

Anyway today I got a TB test so I can participate in a job program. The job program is for people with autism. I recently got marked down for autism on a psych evaluation and I am thankful because not everyone gets their diagnosis. And girls with autism rarely are diagnosed. And people say that it is because it affects girls in a way that is just less bothersome but I am not sure that is the case. I think all these terrible cases of anorexia and cutting and mental illness may be either manifestations of autism or the resulting breakdown from not happily fitting in society and it is a sad, sad thing. And even for me, people might say that I don't need a diagnosis because it is so mild compared to my other mental illness but my other mental illness is probably very much because of the autism and my mental illness is really very tragic. It really is, even though I am happy to be mentally ill because I think mental illness is cool.

But anyway, this weekend I participated in a fundraising walk to help people with developmental disabilities and they gave us pizza and free sandwiches. I think they were mad at me because I did not do that great at volunteering. But I did try my best and I think that ultimately we all have to ask ourselves, okay, does maybe sarah's best not be that great? You know and we have to say okay, does maybe for Sarah, when asked to do a certain work task, for her that means eating a sandwich? I think that is really the direction that treatment and accommodation needs to go in for me.

But anyway, I hope everyone has a Happy Thanksgiving. I am going to volunteer at a hospital for Thanksgiving and I am very excited about it even though you are not supposed to be excited at a hospital.

Association

I am on a trip and on the train we passed an apartment building called Locust Point. Well I am not a marketer but aren't locusts some kind of insect pest? I am just wondering and maybe that helps people sign up for apartments there because they think they might be getting a deal. Or maybe it is from a property company that has two buildings and they named one Locust Point and then charge everyone a million dollars a month at the other one. It's a clever little scheme, really, and it kind of reminds me of a lot of other rent and property schemes, though in NYC I think just the word Locusts is already a reminder of the real estate business.

A Long Post From Some Long Days

Well hi everyone, this is a post I am writing on the train and will post later. I am sitting on the train now in NYC about to leave for Greenville. I am going to an important family occasion. I have not been in a good state of mind for a few days and I have cursed at some people. You are probably saying into your computer, well what seems to be the trouble. Well I will tell you. Friday I was on a subway and thought I was at my stop so I got off the train and then realized it wasn't my stop so I got back on the train but realized I had passed my stop so I needed to get off the train again and the doors were closing so I hurried and held the doors open so I could get through. Well the drivers do not like it when you do that and the guy started closing the door on me repeatedly. Well I have neck problems so that is not good and I chased him down yelling at him as the train was leaving. It was kind of like the Superman scene where Superman runs faster than the train except I did not catch up with the train driver and I was grabbing my neck in exaggerated pain. I do think that train drivers should get in trouble for hurting people on purpose and I told on him. Anyway the next day I volunteered in the Bronx and I was working on a little food task and a guy blasted some embarrassing music right in my ears and it hurt me so much. It made me suicidal and it made me feel like I can never work or volunteer again. But I have volunteered a lot this year and only had a few experiences like that but to me it ruins my life when things like that happen and treatment like that is one of the reasons I haven't been able to work. Anyway I prayed some mean prayers over the weekend and sent a little note about the situation. It is true that addressing things directly usually prevents a lot of resentful grumbling but sometimes it seems impossible to do the confrontations that help you feel okay and prevent further issues.

Anyway, Sunday I had a busy day and then took the guinea pigs to the pet sitter and on the way home I stopped at a restaurant that I had vowed to eat at someday and then I walked on to the train station and gave my leftovers to a guy at the train station. Well it was a great bag of leftovers and I was happy to share except later realized that that guy might have known I had eaten there and been part of some people who tracked me for fifteen blocks to get the food. That sounds paranoid doesn't it? Well a lot of homeless people in New York have certain methods to get cash and they text each other and keep track of who gives what and they conveniently show up in your train car or at certain corners because other people let them know several blocks away that you were walking down the street. Anyway some people in my neighborhood do that to me too and I already have a lot of problems so I am thinking about not giving any food or money to people any more. It is kind of sad because I do think a lot of people not only need but deserve cash handouts but I am not going to reward people for being part of a whole network of people that tracks me and follows me.

Anyway today I went to a certain store that rhymes with "Sold Gravy" (they probably google themselves and sue innocent bloggers) to get some clean pants because the laundromat in my neighborhood got burnt in a fire so I am a little behind on laundry chores. Well they no longer have my size and oddly haven't had my size there since I sent an email complaining about something several months ago. But I don't know if they would have targeted me that much but anyway I ended up getting a pair of "slim" pants and they are horrible! All I can do is be happy for the Wal Mart White Stag brand that now has a chance to really compete based on appearance instead of predatory price slashing and worker's soul slashing. But anyway maybe people won't recognize me in this outfit so they won't be able to target me and keep treating me so bad and hurting me on purpose. I do believe I am on the way to becoming a Batman Villain and it seems that part of my costume will be these horrible slim pants.

These Pants Are Giving Me Dementia

I mention my new pants in the next post also but I just want to say here too that I got some new pants today that aren't the greatest pants I have ever had and I do not feel like myself in them and I am on a train right now and I think I am at risk for wandering off and not knowing who I am. Like I could get off the train at a random stop and not even know my name because these pants are not like the pants that I normally wear. I knew that they would be different because I usually get regular pants but these are slim so they make me look and feel so stupid that I think it could be hard to remember things like my name or my address or something more important which is to never buy these kinds of pants again.

The ghost of Christmas present

Well hi everyone, did y'all have a good Christmas? I had a pretty good Christmas even though I did not send as many gifts to people this year. And I volunteered on Christmas Eve but did not have a good attitude because we had to wash some of the same dishes several times because some people did not do the best they could. But it was probably their way of telling Santa to give their presents to someone else.

Anyway I still have some presents to send to my nieces and just had second thoughts about what I did for them, which was essentially give them each a small suitcase full of one dollar bills, gold one dollar coins, and other mafia reminiscent items like dice and poker chips. It was a fun present, especially since me and my sister grew up watching TV together and have an appreciation for suitcases full of money. But I took apart some cheap metal art cases to do it, and had one for myself which I disassembled today and saw how cool the cases that I took apart were. I mean they were cool art sets, and when I was in town visiting the nieces, I asked them what else they wanted for Christmas, and they said art supplies. So I just had a little section of time where I was questioning my choices, but I think that I did okay and I will send them some art kits soon and send the supplies that I took out of the other art kits.

But anyway, I have discovered in adulthood that one of the great things that you can do is cash out some of your money in one dollar bills and use it to feel rich in different tricky ways. You can do this by carrying a thick wad of money everywhere you go, hiding ones and fives in all your clothes so you are always finding money, or my new favorite, assembling a suitcase full of money as part of your savings plan. It really is just like the TV shows, and even though at Christmas, everyone has just been reminded about how uncool Scrooge is, counting stacks of gold coins is actually almost as satisfying as counting more stacks of gold coins.

Blog Posts from Worldly Monk Theology Blog

Do You See What I See

Here is a blog post that I have been meaning to write for a while. It is about something I recently realized. For years, I have faithfully avoided reading horoscopes or even talking or listening to people who are talking about astrology, because it is not my religion. I am always polite and tell people when I was born and even what my astrological sign is, but I always skip over the horoscope when reading the comics, and was even faithful about this during my most extreme times of doubt and alienation. When all my other Christian habits failed, I just for some reason would not dabble in astrology. And I have really wanted to, and wanted so much to read the horoscope, but I think I caved in only once in about twenty years.

I always did so out of sheer obedience and without much concept of any kind of real consequences or purpose. But in recent years, for some reason, as I have been making choices about what to do next, including big choices like moving to New York City, I have been remembering times even from when I was in college and envisioned the future in certain ways and planned out what would seem right for me to do. And I am really shocked at how vivid my recollections are, and how much I can see the path that was before me and see how much it turned out to be my actual path. I am talking about specific things like working in a bookstore, being a poet, having various levels of leadership and nonleadership, foreseeing suffering and persecution, and all kinds of stuff. I mean it is so clear, and I have ideas about what to do next in my life now, too. And I think that some of what I can see in my mind is probably possible because of a lack of interference from things like astrology. And I can see how if I tried to find out stuff from horoscopes, it really could have confused me.

I have often wondered if maybe people who do psychic readings are often people who just weren't blessed with the same church experiences that I have been, and may even be rewarded by God for using their gifts instead of wasting them, even when their service is technically out of bounds for Christians. And I am also in the camp of people who think that the star the wise men followed in the Bible was something they discovered through astrology.

And yet I am almost shocked and certain to find that my faithfulness that I thought was just for its own sake might be paying off in ways that impact my whole life, and that I have a clear vision of what is expected of me and what has been expected of me in a way that is miraculously not muddied by a half hearted effort that included consulting with the occult or near occult.

It is weird, and if people think that it is just the typical thing that happens to people who were born in the same month as me, please don't tell me, because I don't want to know.

Paper, Rock, Scissors

My reference to there being such thing as a greater life in that other post reminds me of something I was recently thinking about how God uses different kinds of honor to bless people. God tells people more than once in the Bible that people should associate with people of low position, and his disciples have several conversations about who is the greatest. Jesus flips it around sometimes and says that the first shall be last, and he says some hopeful stuff about people being the least. I have found that in life, the best way to treat people is usually to ignore status and to help everyone be loving in a way that rejects meaningless and superficial rankings. And yet there are rankings, and it seems that not all ranking is evil, and there are hierarchies in heaven. I do not know what it all means, except that God flips it around a lot and seems to use a lot of it as a tool to bless people. I also have a current understanding that some of the rankings that are from God and not from the cruel world often have a paper rock scissors relationship, where people might beat someone at something, but that person will beat someone who beats them, and everyone can truly live with the understanding that they can "consider others better than themselves" with relative ease because of people's infinite, immeasurable worth that cannot be confined to lists and position and rankings.

Cracked Reflection

I was thinking just now about how I brag sometimes even though I figured out early in my life that it is basic Christianity not to brag. Well there is a lot I do like that and it is because when I was 19 I found myself looking at a life of severe depression and I decided that I had to just live my life and try for happiness and eat and make friends and do a lot of stuff that is normal human behavior instead of sacrificial Christian living. And yet behind my gregarious selfish extravagance is a very pure Christian motivation to stay alive, not even to have some glorious offering for God, but simply because I am supposed to. And even with my hedonism, which isn't the "Christian hedonism" that some Christians talk about, but just plain hedonism to stay alive, there is an ongoing sacrifice of my reputation among other Christians, who actually don't brag, who don't seek out wordly fame and temporary happiness, who don't depend on accomplishment for self worth, and who serve a lot more people with a lot more purity and holiness. I know how they see me and my moral inferiority, which is real considering my knowledge and training. And yet my participation in the church just can't be the same as theirs. Some people seem to get it even without any explanation from me, and because of them, my little reputation sacrifice and chronic status as an inconsistent and questionable parishoner is, thankfully, limited and minimized so that there are some flashes of service and participation that remind me of life before mental illness. I think all of this must be some kind of help from God that keeps me from becoming a hypocritical monster, and it is something that could provide a great surprise when all the people who did not know to take the glorious Christian path cash in on my prayers that might not have existed if I had been able to truly and successfully walk that path myself.

Bulletin

I think as people read my writing, some of them might find themselves uttering words like "kook." Well I do not mind, but people need to know that kooks might end up being a whole Christian denomination, and I think once mental illness is accounted for, our denomination might really beat all the other denominations at life and Christianity. You know some of the best people from our line of believers actually walk down the street telling people that they are Jesus Christ, and one of the real Jesus Christ's most important messages was that what people do for the least of these, they have done for him. So it would be a little bit crazy to look down on us too much, and it might not be the kind of crazy that counts as membership in our church.

Purgatorio

I think it is time on this blog now to tell everyone that Dorothy Sayers is my patron saint. I made that request a long time ago when I was depressed and working at Barnes and Noble, and continuing to go through a very long Orthodox Christianity phase. The Eastern Orthodox Church is kind of like the Catholic Church where people choose saints to be their patron saints. I knew that I would never be a communing member of the Orthodox Church, so for my patron saint I chose a Christian author that I liked, and who had similar interests as me. Dorothy Sayers was an advertiser before she started writing mysteries, and she was friends with Tolkien and C.S. Lewis. I majored in advertising in college, and I am friends with Jesus Christ. I do not think of those Inklings as often as I used to when working in the bookstore, but I am very blessed in my life and think that Dorothy Sayers was probably not mad about how presumptuous it might have been for me to make a request like that, and to me it seems very likely that she did whatever patron saints do for their assigned people. And she wrote a novel about advertising, and I wrote a novel about advertising, but I did not translate *Dante's Inferno* like she did. When she translated it, she preserved an alternating rhyme scheme in another language. So that is amazing, and I will probably think of her when I am a camp counselor in Purgatory, which I do think will happen, and I will also say in this post that I expect that Mitch McConnell and some other people like that may eventually be some of my campers.

Good Grief

I feel like more and more with media and other things, people have a choice between religion or pornography, when there have been other times when there was more of a variety of things that were just plain good, and when most things in life were more integrated. Some people try to correct the nasty atmosphere with more religious pressure, and then people fight that with more indecency. I think if people would try to grow the amount of goodness and good things and good life then it might also get rid of a lot of the polarization and poverty in our culture.

The miracle of suffering

I have realized sometimes that my survival in life has been somewhat miraculous, and have even had to think about whether there can be such things as twenty-year miracles. I mean in the Bible some of the miracles just took a few minutes and then people enjoyed their health. But when you have a chronic condition and survival really isn't a given, finding yourself to be alive after twenty years of daily suicidal ideation or some other dangerous symptom is really cause for thankfulness and reason to be certain that God has helped you.

But that is not what this post is about. This post is about something else that I don't always think about and will probably immediately retract next time I feel awful. This post is a reflection about what might also be a great miracle, which is the suffering itself.

I am only speaking for myself, though other people might have similar stories. There are mysterious reasons for suffering, and there are benefits that affect other people and can do things like help people know God better or have more compassion. For me personally, I think that some of my suffering has helped me with some of my hypocritical tendencies, and I think that some of the extreme humiliation I have experienced has some kind of value as a Christian witness. Most importantly, I feel securely able to pray to God as much as I want and have gotten to know him better. There are probably other benefits, too. But even that is still not exactly what I am saying is a miracle.

What I am really saying is that it is a miracle that someone like me could suffer at all. I just grew up in a great environment with awesome friends and cash for great grocery stores, and parents who cared and provided for me, but who weren't necessarily eager to support me as some kind of life-risking Christian missionary. When you have blessings and resources like I had, which included getting to go to college and having a lot of opportunities and good health, then it really usually is morally questionable to just waste that stuff for suffering's sake. I wouldn't be allowed to go to some dangerous place to live for a worthy cause, and it would be an intolerable offense to try to replicate those conditions in my own life, so what are my options? Well good service and giving for other people are great options. They really are and I will always tell people who feel happy and well to make the most of their blessings and don't underestimate what people can accomplish by helping others and being honest and good.

But for me, I was interested in some of the more extreme messages about the cross of Christ, and it seemed like that kind of adventure might have been intended for other people. However, I think that is not what happened. I have had a great opportunity to feel worn out, to forgive, to show up and be a part of other people's lives despite pain, and, well, to wish I was dead for years at a time. And how stupid to call that a miracle, but how stupid not to, because God has been good to me, and though I deserved to be treated better in life, I got better than what I deserved.

What if I did say this

Something I have been saying lately is "I did not do or say that but what if I did." It is a little something that I thought up because people try to get on everyone's case about every little mistake, and I am saying what if I do say the wrong thing and even what if I do have some character problems? You know, what if I do? Everyone has to get out and live their lives without being perfect and it is a brave thing to do. And as the flaws increase, the courage to face the world anyway increases, which is not something to feel bad about.

Because or despite

This is a post that could go on my mental health blog and I might do another one like it for that list of posts. I am just thinking about friends from a long time ago who were there for me, and I have to say that church people have really not let me down, even after sometimes being taught that people like me are bad people. It is common for people with mental illness and problems like that to be misunderstood and rejected for bad reasons, which has happened to me and a lot of other people, and has happened in church settings. But literally hundreds of church people have come through for me and included me in their dearest groups of friends. There have been times where I could barely have a conversation with people and could barely even sit up or hear what other people were saying. But some of the greatest people in the world became my sincere friends. I have tried to do that for others, and I would say that friendship with me is not usually complete charity. But when it has been kind of like that, people did come through. There is still no excuse for pastors to teach that mental illness is sin, or that people who take medicine for depression might not be real Christians, but the consistent help and "inclusion anyway" from their congregations is not something to be overlooked when looking at how the church treats suffering people.

Just Like in the cartoons

One of the most interesting and important ideas of Christianity and really a moral law of the universe, is that "He who loses his life for Christ will save it, and he who tries to save his life will lose it." It is something that happens in big and small ways and could be part of scenarios like letting someone have the last piece of dessert and then that is right when someone brings out a better dessert that you get to have. That is kind of a stupid example but there really are ways that unselfishness pays off in little moments and in great spans of history or just across a lifetime. It has kind of driven me crazy to try not to be on the losing side of that principle, but I think letting my OCD kick in to obsessively try not to lose anything actually would be one of the instances where I end up losing instead of gaining.

But anyway the thing I want to mention about it is something that I had to learn pretty early on in my life, which is that things can be confusing when there are situations where you really do need to save your life or someone else's. That is what happened to me when depression threatened to win out and made me suicidal. I abruptly had to stop looking for opportunities to suffer on purpose and started having to do everything to hoard as much happiness as I could find. It changed the way I interacted with people and looked at friendship, and ironically, I think that it helped me be a truer friend instead of looking at people as potential good deeds. Probably that whole idea of going ahead and losing some Christianity points and choosing some kind of authentic life actually is just another basic example of saving your life by losing it, but it is disguised, because didn't I save my life by saving it?

God is very clever and He is the one who saves with all of his laws of nature and with all of his intervention beyond those laws. Everyone who trusts in him is guaranteed to be in what basically amounts to a Scooby Doo episode where at the end the villains will say, "Curses, foiled again." Even those of us who start paying attention to all the patterns around us and trying to deliberately beat the system are like simple Looney Tunes road runners who just go where we are going while all the evil coyote plans backfire all around us. And in the end, we will be winners, diving into piles of gold like Scrooge McDuck and his nephews in the Ducktales cartoon.

Ironically

Well everyone, in this blog I have repeated some of my ideas that I have used before in poems and sayings, but I think it could be good that I keep coming back to some recurring themes. That could be how I know that I am onto something important. This particular thing that I want to mention has to do with some of my thoughts about staying alive, and what to think when life becomes a lot about endurance instead of blessings or even service and productivity. I have been truly miserable sometimes with no end in sight, and it made me wonder what the purpose of living is. I mean why should people be able to take away my Christian martyrdom AND get away with torturing me. It seems like it should be one or the other. Like you can't make my life meaningless and purposeless and be allowed to hurt me on purpose. And yet I have found myself in situations that seem like that. I have tried to handle those situations by praying more, thinking that maybe my prayers would count for more since I did not feel good, but it is hard to believe that kind of thing when you feel like your life is being wasted. However, after years of doing what therapists call "Opposite action," where you just keep building a life when you don't feel like it, I have concluded that the very times that most seem like lose-lose situations are actually part of a life that has a bright side on every side. I have concluded that if I am expected to keep living with unbearable suffering, then my existence must be very important and every second that I spend on earth is crucial. And then the other bright side is that if people, including me, really are allowed to ruin my life, then that must mean that the most important stuff is in heaven, and I can accept extreme losses here with infinite hope. It is kind of a luxury to write about this stuff now that some of my suffering has eased up and I don't have to be using all my might to get through each day, but I think there is a reverse alternative to thinking okay, people are allowed to take away both my temporal happiness and my eternal reward. It's more like all the swindling and adversity can both confirm the once-in-eternity nature of this opportunity to live, and still suggest that there must be some kind of consolation so great that people can take it all and they have taken nothing.

Christian Agnosticism

I have been thinking about converting to Catholicism lately, but can never quite let go of being an Evangelical, and then other feelings of confusion kick in and I am left with the same exasperation where I feel responsible for sharing all my faith but don't know what that is. I mean the gospel as I know it is now a fifty volume mess of thoughts from reading a thousand books and learning from hundreds of friends who believe different things. And the gospel as I don't know it is a million books plus the religion I was taught by people who turned out to be chronically wrong about many important things that it is really not okay to still be wrong about.

So I am wondering if I should just continue my constant obsessive code cracking and say whatever happens to be my belief at whatever time, or if maybe I should simplify things and give myself a little label like Christian Agnostic. I probably shouldn't, since people might think I do not believe in God and Jesus, when really, I feel very thankful to not just believe in God but to know him personally and be one of his friends. And I know all along the way that God has wanted me to do things the way He would do it, and one of those things is being friends with agnostics. So maybe that means God might want a little friend who doesn't know everything, and maybe that person is me.

Stages of Faith

I think some people think that to be religious at all is to automatically be a hypocrit, and there is just no such thing as true Christianity and a good person who has faith. But a lot of the people who promote those accusations are often the people who have created a culture so vile that basic human decency and honesty might really become impossible standards, and where the people who have Christian morals aren't allowed to follow through on their beliefs and therefore are constantly tempted to pretend to achieve Christian ideals anyway. A lot of people who call us hypocrits have truly made it impossible for us to succeed at our faith by deliberately corrupting every system that we have to be a part of to stay alive. So we are stuck with a choice to either be honest animals or fake saints, where we at least give some kind of shout out to what we were striving for by doing some pretending here and there.

I also think in times that Christians fall short and truly do show some hypocritical tendencies, like when we choose to use people and "turn in" unbelievers to churches by showing everyone how we are reaching out to people, that this kind of unacceptable behavior is often just a phase or stage of growth on a path that in the big picture is actually very glorious and the victims of our two-faced double-dealing are actually still indebted to have any inkling at all of the mere existence of church and Christian truth. I mean I say that knowing full well that stench is stench and people are right to be disgusted by fake friendship and condescension, but we should protect ourselves and everyone around us from the lies of the media, or literature, and of academic people who invest so much effort in trying to convince people that Christians are the ones who are perpetually dishonest. I hope that maybe somewhere quiet in people's minds, they have the strength to do the math, and to think to themselves, "okay, what is really suspicious here? Is it the people who praised sobriety but couldn't help but party a little too hard with people they love? Or is it the people who brag about reading *Lolita* and mock autistic homeschool children because they said they are thankful to be forgiven for their sins? I think in the end, it is most questionable to try to block a door to heaven, and quite hypocritical, too, since it is impossible to close a door held open by two hands that have nails through them.

Ideas

I think that when things really get bad in a country, and there is mass stupidity on a scale that threatens to take the whole country down, one option is for the country to divide itself into two countries and let people choose whether they want to be in "The Good Country," or "The Bad Country." Well who would want to be in a bad country? Only stupid people. So they can make their choice, and our work is done here. That is kind of how heaven and hell works, and the strategy might work well on earth sometimes, too.

A winning war strategy is to have already won

There is a verse in the Bible that I think Jesus says, which is to be "shrewd as serpents and innocent as doves." It is a clear instruction for everyone to think smart and deliberately participate in the outwitting of the demons. However, I think that in a society that is even remotely fair, people should not have to be geniuses to do what they are supposed to and live a decent life. If basic honesty and kindness are thwarted at every step, then the bad people's evil schemes are embarrassingly complicated and they are the ones with the problem. In situations where a general and faithful goodness is not allowed, then a certain martyrdom or partial martyrdom will characterize the lives of those who are disappointed to not be their best selves, and we will be surprised at the end when the blame we expect turns to credit.

Another thought I have about how much strategy it should take to obey God is that when people do what they are supposed to and live according to the Holy Spirit, then our normal actions and words become apt and fitting in a way that is backed by God's authorial genius and take on a quality of cleverness that can be a thousand times what we would imagine on purpose. With all of God's literary devices and engineering of physical laws, when we tell the truth and merely agree to follow the command to "let your yes be yes and your no be no," our simple words can instantly be the wittiest sayings imaginable and our deeds become part of an unstoppable and unprecedented master plan.

With a vengeance

Ok everyone, I thought of a theological question that I think is one of my most interesting wonderings. You know how people always say that one of the reasons to forgive and not seek retaliation about things is because God says "Vengeance is mine. I will repay." People quote that a lot and sometimes use it to encourage people not to seek some kind of justice or revenge, and people make it sound like those are the same things. But yesterday I was thinking about it and don't people also spend their whole lives trying to be "Godly" and do everything according to how God himself would do it? That is the idea of following Jesus Christ, and of being "imitators of God." So my question is this: wouldn't that mean sometimes saying "Vengeance is mine, I will repay?" I just know everyone is saying, "Of course not," but isn't the real answer "Of Course?" I am genuinely wondering because I definitely in recent years have found more of an appreciation for people who stand up to evil and abuse and make reputation sacrifices to be the ones to say we are not going to tolerate scams and abuse.

I think that is really almost enough to say but it makes me pause to think about the cross again, which is such a symbol of forgiveness, but also was a deliberate act that was defended by the presence of swords in the garden of Gethsemane. Why did the disciples have swords if it was all about letting people abuse Christ? To me there is a case that Christ went to the cross deliberately for a lot of reasons, and there might have been more of an offensive (like basketball offense) strategy not just against evil itself but against specific evil people throughout all of history who have been and still are very defeated by the cross and by all of the believers who learn to literally fight for all kinds of salvation and freedom.

The twelve doofuses

Sometimes when the disciples of Christ messed up in the Bible, Jesus would say stuff like "Are you still so dull?" and the equivalent of "How can you be so stupid?" and I think a lot of people see it and find it to be a surprisingly gruff manner from someone who would eventually forgive people while being tortured on a cross. In fact, I even read a book where an important theologian practically called Jesus a jerk for talking to people that way. But we know that he wasn't a jerk, so what does it all mean? Well I had an idea yesterday while imagining myself helping people not miss out on Christianity which is that his emphatic rebukes to people who were already so rich as to be in the company of Christ himself and have since then inherited an eternal honor almost beyond comprehension is that one of the reasons he was tough on people is because the stakes were so high and there was a great reward that he did not want them to miss out on. And it is an indication to everyone, including people now, that we should not be stupid and constantly promote our own greatness in a way that makes us miss out on greater glory and love. I also think that it is an example of how to live, much in the same way that all his kinder words were, and that when we think things like, "Why would anyone do drugs instead of working?" or "How can people be so stupid to think all the planets just appeared out of nowhere and all the animals invented themselves through mutation?" that there may be some occasions where this exasperation should be expressed in full. And that the main goal is not our own vain desires to be known as people who are generally right about everything, but that there is some blessing available that we would not want anyone to miss out on, especially if we have any influence over them, even as persecuted people who don't have the greatest media power.

Disclaimer

I feel like writing a little disclaimer on this blog, because I have recently ventured into theological territory that really does matter for people and can be controversial not in a random political conversation way but in a way where I really don't want to mislead people about stuff that can affect their whole lives. So my disclaimer is to say that I really think some sermons and ideas from the Bible are medicine for people's souls, but that this blog is really more like food and not medicine. It is a leftover squash casserole from Thanksgiving, and not a potent dose of healing medicine which people might really get from a church with people who have not had as many thoughts so muddled by entire bookstores of other ideas and conversations with people who believe other stuff and who I wanted to like me. I called this blog the Worldly Monk Theology Blog because my life is a mix of very strict religious loyalty and prayer but also a very liberal participation in a messy world and a filthy, lost, abused and abusive culture.

AA Post

A story that really affected me in a profound way and something that I think of pretty often is one of the stories behind the beginning of Alcoholics Anonymous, which is an organization that I find heroic and miraculous. It is a story about part of the experience of Bill W., who had terrible problems as an alcoholic, and who one day reportedly said, "If there is a God, let him show himself." And soon after that, Bill W started Alcoholics Anonymous, which has helped thousands of people overcome addiction and find support during tragic suffering. People in the group rely on their "Higher Power," and while many people take a conspicuously great effort to point out that Alcoholics Anonymous is not the church, it seems pretty obvious that God himself has intervened continuously through AA from the very beginning.

That utterance or something like a prayer that is so out of bounds for most people is so amazing to me, and the story inspires me, because it seems just like God to answer just that kind of "prayer," and maybe even to wait for that kind of request that so much reflects the desperation of someone suffering from alcohol addiction. I could go on and on about it and I am tempted to just translate all my prayers into that format. Like... if God wants me to do my impossible chores, let him show himself. And if God wants me to stop cursing at people, let him show himself.

But this blog post is about something entirely different, and it is a topic where I really have decided that I might adopt that Bill W prayer mindset about something that has been driving me crazy quite literally for many years. It has to do with Presbyterian Theology, and how much I do and don't believe it, and what exactly I am supposed to take into the world as a mission when I can't quite be certain of almost everything anyone has ever said to me.

I said in another post that I have some Catholic leanings, and some of that is from wanting to believe that there is a more specific application of an all inclusive mercy and justice for people and an ongoing opportunity for anyone to know God personally instead of an all or nothing theology test where if you pray a certain prayer then you escape eternal torture. I change my mind a lot and actually have learned to just keep myself from obsessing about it and try to be productive in other ways, but I can't quite ever fully escape the ideas I have been taught, and the belief that it must be resolved and might even be the only thing that matters for anyone. Even as I say that, it sounds so absurd, and yet many books in the New Testament support some of that teaching, along with the idea that everything has been predetermined with a good God behind everything that happens. I do find myself thinking that people are pretty stupid to try to do everything good except ask God for Christ's forgiveness. I mean, how insulting to someone who died to save people from their sins.

But I still waver all the time and thought recently that I might be able to find some temporary peace and another segment of time where I can keep living life without all the answers if I officially shrug off the burden of being responsible for everyone else, and if I shrug off the pressure of having to believe something that I can't go that long of a time believing. I think that Bill W's prayer could be the key, and I could just say even after all the revelation from church and time, if the Presbyterians were ever right, let God be the one to say it, and let the Protestant theology show itself. God can make the sky plaid if he wants, or drop a stone tablet on my head that has the Westminster Confession carved into it, or drop stone tablets on the people who are mean to me at the grocery store, or send an alcoholic missionary to help me decide that I do not have to be the one to save everyone.

Mental Health Blog intro

Well everyone, I am starting a new blog about mental health. It is crazy to think that this could become the main way I share my ideas and stories about living with mental illness, because I have a lot to say and have had some crazy experiences and some experiences just being crazy. You really aren't supposed to refer to people as crazy, and some would say don't call yourself that either, but I have always been pretty happy to be in that category.

I remember when I was in elementary school, we had field day each year right before school was out, and the fifth graders always did a certain relay called "the String Man," which involved choosing one person from your team to stand at the end of the field and then everyone took turns running to put oversized crazy clothes on them, like a hat and a tie and a giant coat, and for the finale, a ping pong ball in the mouth. Even though I was a little scared of the ping pong ball requirement, I always wanted to be the String Man, and when I was finally in fifth grade, my dream came true and my group let me be the String Man. It was an honor to be the crazy person in front of everyone, and I mostly feel the same way about my mental illness now. Different people have had different experiences with losing their minds, and mental illness is often a path of continual heartbreak and humiliation. So I do not want to come across in any insensitive way or make light of people's pain. But I genuinely have always thought mentally ill people were cool and interesting, and I am overjoyed and thankful beyond any capability of expressing it to live almost my whole life with a mind that makes mood rings shoot sparks and that keeps reality from dominating every conversation like I do when I am manic.

I am a fool and a weirdo, and sometimes an outcast, and sometimes a spectacle, but every day I generate more prayer and ideas, more material for comedy in heaven, more potential friendship for others who suffer, and most importantly, most nobly, and most spiritually... carbon dioxide. Just staying alive is literally a lifetime achievement accomplished every day. Reality is different for mentally ill people, and not just because of delusions. During a depression, microwaving a bag of popcorn can become a heroic act of strength, and for someone with social anxiety, looking out the window can be a triumph. Our suffering is a mystery to some of the sanest, smartest people there are, and as we endure our hardship while being so often misunderstood, there are opportunities for great wisdom found in mental spaces that most people will never have access to. Some of those spaces happen to be hell on earth for years at a time, so let's not paint a picture that is too optimistic. But let's do paint some pictures and eat some good food and keep on going just in case we have a day where we find that we are the people responsible for telling the people who judge us that they are raving lunatics.

Some people get to go to McDonalds after the hospital

Well everyone, for this post, I am going to share my favorite term that I learned from social work school, which I completed in 2016. The term is "disenfranchised grief." I think that one of the most talked about ideas right now is the idea of "privilege," which has to do with unrightful societal benefits. That wasn't really the idea that most resonated in my soul, but when I stumbled upon the term "disenfranchised grief" in an article about people who have had to go to jail, I felt that years of thinking had finally found a representation in another context. The term has also been used in other articles, and I think it was first thought of by someone named Doka in 1989. It was weird for it to be just a sidebar that I gleaned from reading about other topics, because to me it almost epitomizes what I think is a core struggle for all kinds people, including everyone who is hurt by things like privilege.

Disenfranchised grief refers to the uncomforted mourning of people who have losses and suffering that the people around them and the rest of the society either do not care about or do not understand. I think almost everyone can relate, but for some people, it is a defining feature of their whole lives or of certain major experiences. People with addictions often have loss upon loss and not only have no sympathy, but take a lot of blame for their problems which happened from a spiral that at some point, they had little control to prevent. Legal troubles and going to jail or being in the military and having family life disrupted can be situations that are disenfranchised, or even "anti-franchised," though people in the military are often called heroes and there might be some support that others might not have.

Really, anyone in any situation can find their pain deemed irrelevant by other people when it is never mentioned in church sermons, or never mentioned in the media, and when personally no friends seem to truly be there for them.

I think that even with this concept that almost anyone can probably relate to on some level, there are people who seek out those who need consolation, and a lot of people can eventually find someone who cares and understands. I think that is what social work and mental health services are really about, and I remember getting training for a Crisis Line and the leader told us that what counts as a crisis is different for different people. I mean that is so simple and yet it is so foundational if people really want to show any kind of compassion for anyone else in the world.

I wanted to share it on my blog early on, because I think even the existence of a term like that reverses some of the damage and offers "franchise" both to all the neglected losses, and to the additional heartbreak of disenfranchised grief itself.

Mental health certificates

I would like to share an idea that I think is already happening in some ways, which is for there to be more programs that offer mental health certificates, peer counseling credentials, and other mental health degrees that can be earned by people who have learned about mental health through suffering and survival, such as through a lifetime of managing mental illness symptoms or trying to heal from trauma or grief. I think it is a well known fact that many people who have struggled with almost any kind of emotional pain do find their way into the social work field and medical field as helpers, and one of my therapists from a long time ago said that therapists were often called "wounded healers." It is true, and maybe no one needs to say it, but I have gotten the impression that there are a lot of mentally ill people out there who take their medicine, sometimes post comments on website discussions, may or may not have a part time job or hobby, but have no real formal recognition of the mental work they have had to do and the conundrums they have had to figure out in order to survive. I mean just a class, or a few classes, or a year long program that helps them meet other people, could help them end up with a great certificate or degree to feel good about and possibly to help them find another official opportunity to share their life and learning with others who might be just beginning to navigate the challenges of depression and anxiety or other disorders. Some group outpatient programs might consider offering an education component like that, too, which also incentivizes continuing treatment. It is also an alternative to putting a diagnosis on a resume, which is another thing that people might consider more often. The fact is that patients themselves often do not realize what kind of accomplishment is mixed in with all the days of sleeping late, going places when you don't feel like it, and drinking extra coffee, and a certificate on the wall could really be a reminder that at least some people have some idea of their true success.

Seen and unseen

There is a book called *Blindness*, by a guy named Saramago, or maybe a movie that I am getting it confused with, but basically the concept is that everyone goes blind except this one lady who can still see and she gets mixed in with all the blind people and is able to help them because of her sight. I really liked the book and was thinking the other day that some of my experience with mental illness is like being both a blind person and the seeing person in that same scenario. And it might not be my mental illness as much as it is an Asperger's profile with extreme gifts and extreme deficits. Basically what happens is that I am a terrible helpless mess a lot of the times, but also a very capable strong person who can save the day for everyone around me. There are days and times where I lean more in one direction, but mostly I am just a mix of these things every day. And the effect it has is that I see for myself how disabled people are treated, but I know the cost and intent of that treatment as someone who is also not disabled. I could probably write a much more thorough essay with examples, but I think that just mentioning it is enough for now. I think in a way we all have kind of a spy quality to us as humans, and Christ himself said that what you do for the least of these is what you do for him. So people are all kind of in a Shakespearian *Twelfth Night* play where people's true identity is eventually revealed and justice happens as people are exposed in their compassion or snobbery. But I do think that there is some weird way where as a mentally ill person I experience this more than normal, and I see people include me with strength that I have used for other people before, or I see people dismiss me or even abuse me when they do not know what kind of insight I have into their absolute hypocrisy.

Suicidal Prayer Credit

I think many people will say I am wrong about this and that it is bad theology but I think I am right enough to give people this idea so that they can have the same hope and endurance that has benefitted me. The idea that I am sharing is simple, which is that if people have lived through any amount of suicidal thinking, it might be a good idea to just pray even a few of the biggest prayers you can think of for everyone you know and for your society because it could be a very special thing that you are still alive, and this might add some power to your prayers. That is where people say okay no wait a minute you don't earn prayer power through your own efforts but I am not sure everyone really knows how everything works and I think once there have been significant threats to people's survival, and especially a chronic danger or a questioning of whether it is worth it to go on, then that is a clue that people's mere presence and existence is not something to take for granted, and just the effort of a few extra moments of thoughtfulness might be something that God is willing to match a millionfold. Is that so weird? I am saying that when I have gotten through or am even in the middle of discouragement so bad that I think I can't go on, it takes five seconds to ask God for a million feasts and forgiveness for everyone who has ever lived. I mean it is times like that when you ask for salvation for all mankind, or for everyone ever to have the relief that you can no longer even imagine. Do other people not have a hunch that their prayers might be worth a little extra after twenty years of struggling to stay alive? It actually is hard to do sometimes, because depression so often brings a feeling of being so bad that God would never answer any prayers. But couldn't the suffering also be proof that something good is at risk, and might that thing be something as simple as one little prayer prayed for everyone at the right time? I do not think I will ever regret trying to add prayer to my despair.

Help for Future Wounds

I am just telling this little story because I think it is interesting. I recently bought a roll of gauze at the drug store for a wound on my hand, but then the wound healed and I did not need the gauze. And when I was straightening up my apartment and found the gauze that I no longer needed, I started thinking that maybe God knows that I am going to have a gash my hand in the future and that is why he arranged for me to have some gauze on hand. Get it? On hand? But anyway I am saying what if the whole reason I got the gauze was for another injury coming soon. Like a guaranteed gash on my hand that could happen any day and is part of destiny. It made me feel scared, and then I figured out that I was being a little bit mentally ill and those thoughts were irrational. I think it is kind of an interesting story, because people do have illogical worrying sometimes, and I think it is good for me to catch myself doing it because a lot of my worrying doesn't seem illogical.

Hyper Abuse

Ok everyone, here is the post that everyone has been vigilantly waiting for: a post about vigilance, and maybe even hyper vigilance. Hyper-vigilance is a type of anxiety problem and a symptom of trauma. A lot of people talk about it in the context of PTSD when something horrible has happened and from then on the people who suffered are constantly on the lookout to protect themselves from anything else like it. But I want to say that a lot of people are in chronic stress situations that do warrant some kind of unreasonable vigilance, so people's anxiety can be both appropriate and inappropriate at the same time. I consider myself to have been in situations like this for decades at a time, and I may never really understand why that turned out to be part of my life. For me, it was the stress of being mentally ill and keeping a retail job where any wrong move or bad word could cost me medical insurance for the rest of my life, and result in homelessness, death, or bankruptcy, and in my mind, cause a subsequent loss of the ultimate privilege of pleasing God with a productive Christian life. Other people find themselves in situations that I think extract even more of a constant vigilance, such as caring for children with special needs, or caring for children at all in such a dangerous culture and world. It is wearing on people in ways that I think no one else ever understands, even when other people are living their own lives of hyper-vigilance. And I think that it can be confusing when there are official mental health symptom labels that by definition suggest that maybe some vigilance isn't justified, though most people assessing those symptoms usually do have some clue about the true suffering. But what I am saying is that people are misunderstood when the unreasonableness of the persecution or the excessive responsibility makes people think that the emotional reaction of total fear or constant alertness is what is unreasonable. Frankly, church people make this mistake very often, and I also think a lot of mindfulness people who lead meditations where they literally say things like "you have no problems" and "everything is how it is meant to be" are even worse than the bad Christian counselors. But the fact is that you are supposed to be scared when a giant python is squeezing the life out of you or your loved ones, or when a society of thousands gang up on you to take everything you have as soon as you acquire anything, or when an evil government holds your people hostage and grants little moments of relief in exchange for a gradual compromise of everything you believe in. Some evil warrants sheer terror, and some people are terrorized not just in horrible events but in their everyday lives for years. People who say that there's nothing to worry about are unworthy of what has been preserved by the monitoring and endurance of depressed people, and many of us have been so burnt by our own brain chemicals that we simply don't have any energy left to feel sorry for the shamefully ignorant people who told us that it was a sin to be anxious.

Dogs Know

I am putting this post on the mental health blog, because I do not mean for it to be argumentative. It is just something that I want to say about animals and people. And I am not just sharing an opinion, but speaking from years of experience as a person with depression and anxiety, and as a person who aspires to eventually do some pet therapy with my pet guinea pigs.

A lot of people like to talk about how animals have an extra sense about things, and can sometimes perceive when something is wrong, or when there is a person who means harm. Well it is true and family dogs save the day all the time, and service dogs defend their dog owners from bothersome encounters very often.

But I think that healthy people who don't have a deep experience of chronic rejection and emotional pain may not realize that dogs do not know everything, and just because a dog barks at you doesn't mean that you are a bad person. And telling everyone that this is the case may really hurt people. Some people already feel like bad people when they aren't, and when some grumpy dog barks at them, that's all it is. The dog has not discovered the true nature of anyone's character. And there are mean dogs who attack children in neighborhoods every day. And who is the bad person in that scenario? Usually a bad neighbor who didn't give a flip about anyone else's safety, though of course sometimes there are genuine tragedies and accidents.

Especially in my early years of depression, I found myself feeling a fear of being unliked by dogs many times, and feeling that based on other people's belief that dogs are the ultimate judge of character, and that if a dog growls at me then everyone has the right to conclude that I am really a bad person. In reality, the dog might just sense my fear... of seeming like a bad person... because I am a good person who is taking a risk by being near an animal in a social situation.

I am not making a big deal of it, but I have never heard anyone call people out on this whole gleeful suggestion that dogs make the final call on the state of people's hearts. It is something that healthy people who aren't scared of having their feelings hurt by a dog take for granted, and it is something that no one understands until they have had social status so low that to be merely ignored by someone's dog can be the final proclamation of their guilt and worthlessness.

Lowerarchies

In my early years of mental illness, I was in agony all the time but was able to hide a lot of my illness to the point where a lot of people just thought I was some kind of selfish loser with a bad attitude. I always kind of wished that I had less pain and more visible symptoms so I could get credit for being mentally ill but felt better. My illness now is a little bit like that, and though I am definitely heartbroken about a lot of it, I would like to say that I was kind of right about some of the way I thought that it might be nicer to have a more obvious illness with less pain. And my symptoms now are very crazy schizophrenia symptoms that are considered by many to objectively be the worst mental illness that a person can have. But as a person with that privileged status, I would like to say that any mental illness and even heartbreak that isn't mental illness can zap people as much as any other category. Depression and anxiety seem so normal, almost like healthy human emotions, but they can both be entire disorders that devastate people beyond comprehension. I have had all kinds of different depression feelings before, and some different kinds of anxiety, and I just want to say that they are not lesser mental illnesses in any way than the stuff that makes me talk to myself and hit myself in the middle of a job interview. And I still think no matter what I say, people will never understand how painful depression can be, and how debilitating anxiety can be, but I will still say that if people tell me they are so sorry that I have schizoaffective disorder and a whole mess of other symptoms, I might genuinely say sometimes, that "at least it's not PMS."

A helpful OCD and Psychosis Intervention

I am putting this post on my mental health blog even though to me it really could be on the theology blog. This post is about one of my strategies that helps me get through situations when I feel like I fall short of important standards in front of everyone. A lot of behavior details matter to me, and I do think that small interactions can be very important and very representative of people's character and regard for other people. But I do have some crazy neurosis and psychosis, so when I go wrong on a little detail and say the wrong thing or don't stick up for my faith and beliefs, or give a false impression or forget something important, I feel terrible and also feel ashamed in front of imagined onlookers who probably have their own goals to think about. It is a recipe for torment, but I have found a great mental and spiritual solution that works almost every time to help me accept my imperfections. The thing that works is simply taking a few moments to think of letting someone else get the honor that I would have gotten for keeping certain standards. You know, for everything I get wrong, there are people who would and who do get it right, and who don't bail on people and don't let people get picked on in their presence, and who do a better job of reporting suspicious packages at the subway. So when I fail, I have found that because I am so driven to be perfect, I actually can understand and feel happy for other people who actually achieve that vision, and I can successfully console myself by thinking about someone else getting some kind of glory, and some kind of reward, and some kind of credit in our world or even on the actual Judgment Day in heaven. Some of this could be material for comedy, but to me it is a serious thing deep in my heart and I am thankful to be able to get such relief for every failure and to know that some of the service in the world and the good deeds from each other that we all rely on and sometimes take for granted are actually not that easy. And failure is a reminder of the cost of all the successes, and a comforting guarantee that I can look forward to other people's rewards as much as my own.

Good Mourning

A friend of mine's stepmom once said that she thought that Post Traumatic Stress Disorder should be called Post Traumatic Stress "Order" because of course people would have nervous breakdowns from such horrible experiences. And as much as I do think mental disorders mostly truly are disorders and medical conditions, I occasionally go ahead and let myself think about life and conclude that any amount of broken mindedness and broken heartedness is not only appropriate in this sad world but possibly the only right state of mind. I mean, for people to read the news and somehow live on without severe depression must be some kind of mental illness that they should be institutionalized for. And I even see a case for thinking that the most outrageous delusions and hallucinations might arise from a very accurate assessment of a reality that is too tragic to accept at face value. I don't mean to sound like I am wishing panic attacks on people, because of course I am not, but I think that every now and then it might be good for everyone to go ahead and admit that it does seem like a lot of the people in the mental hospitals are the ones who really seem to "get it" and understand life with all its heart wrenching ways.

Big Picture Strategies

This idea is, like a few other posts, something that could go on the theology blog, but I am putting it on the mental health blog because I think that it could especially help people who have trouble with some of their goals and skills of living because of mental illness. And sometimes some of the troubles people have are because of their mental illness and they don't know it, like feelings of laziness and undone chores, or habits that people can't seem to break.

But anyway, in my twenties, I felt like such a failure all the time and there were so many things that I just couldn't fix. For instance, my car was messy for all the years I had a car, and I could rarely have passengers. I also have had trouble eating well and often found myself eating fast food or frozen meals that I didn't really want instead of taking the time to cook, or sometimes, I felt like I splurged on groceries to cook when I should have eaten a frozen meal. I mean some of that is just always feeling like I could never do anything right when really it was probably okay to just eat whatever I could.

But anyway, I mention those examples because those categories where people like me feel like we can't ever get anything right do add up and make us feel like we can't accomplish anything. And having OCD just makes people more scrupulous about everything, including religion and socializing.

But I found that especially because of working and going to school, that what I would call "big picture" interventions or some kind of large framework activity, totally changed my life, helped me be a generally more productive person, and took my mind off the details. It is as simple as saying that I kept a job and did some school programs. Maybe it would be better to say it that way than making it sound like some kind of advanced mental health strategy, but I do think there is something about the structural nature of what helped me that is good to share for people who get trapped trying to improve their lives in perpetually microscopic ways that never quite work out.

What I am saying is that some of those microscopic things get worked out automatically when there are bigger goals that people actually care about, like art, or writing poetry, or being part of a sports team or writing group, or doing some kind of volunteer work. And I also found that some of my smaller self-improvement goals really were impossible, and I let them go. I was more able to accept my imperfections (which actually are pretty significant) because I had other stuff going for me. And I think a lot of people might say, well, hmm, I think it might have been better to go ahead and keep a clean room or eat less sugar or read the Bible in less haphazard ways, but I want to say that really there aren't that many critics who really do have other people's foibles and faults on their list of things to worry about, and nothing has helped me more than signing up for school and going to classes and making a few bigger decisions that result in some of my life schedule already being decided for a while. The big goals also help distract me from depression and suicidal thinking, and while so many people don't have money for extravagant education , or access to a broad selection of arts programming that they can be a part of, it is likely that there is some kind of thing, whether it is church or volunteering or a mental health group, that can be worked in to people's lives so they set their alarm at 10 am for a purpose instead of setting their alarm at 6 am to try to prove to themselves and to the wind that they are still disciplined.

Advice: People who do not live in glass houses should throw stones.

I am currently finishing a book and want to be done but have one more blog post to add to my mental health blog. I just want to say something that I recently figured out, which is something that is different than some of my thinking was for a while. What I am talking about is self-improvement advice that is designed for people with healthy minds. There are a lot of sayings about how everything comes down to having a good attitude, and there is writing that praises cheerfulness, and advice about efficiency and not wasting time and all kinds of suggestions for people to be successful literally in every moment of their days. And over the years, I have read some of these books, and some of these facebook posts, and heard some of these sermon references and thought, okay, that is great, but they clearly just don't understand. They just don't understand what it is like to truly be human which I define as crawling into a corner crying every day.

But I recently grew a little bit in my thinking, and realized that it is a little bit self-absorbed of me to think that everyone else who is striving to have a meaningful life and do good or even great things needs to tailor every message to those of us who have debilitating mental illness.

The fact is that people who have strong minds should also play to their strengths, which literally could be everything they do, and they should be free and inspired to achieve all they can and boldly fling any perpetual good attitude in this oppressive world's face. All of us are dependent on those superstars, and why should they wallow in the self-pity of others. It is absurd, and when I read the encouraging advice that is for them and even might seem insensitive to my own ongoing loss that comes with depression and okay, psychosis, then I will be happy for them and be thankful that they are giving their all. It is not fair for me to think less of people who waste their sanity and then also look down on people who have the luxury not having to waste anything. So when people say on facebook that attitude is everything, or that making their bed is the key to a successful life, I am going to be thankful that I live in the same world with those people, and that they have included me to the extent that I can overhear any of their conversations about their clean and good habits that allow them to accomplish the most extreme human achievements, like writing thank you notes, having friends ride in their cars, and having clean dishes to eat off of. That sounded sarcastic, but it isn't sarcastic, which probably matches some great advice out there that I don't know about because it wasn't posted on a Starbucks cup or Coke can.

Mad Blog Posts

My Opinion about USA Healthcare

The healthcare problems are about ten scams combined:

-Drug companies and medical services gouging everyone
-A layer of absurdly high insurance profit on a pooled-money cost-sharing system
-Insurance companies taking money and not providing coverage
-Discrimination against the sick and disabled through pre-existing conditions coverage denial and enslaving policies requiring continuation of coverage
-Employer based insurance instead of true free market individual insurance for anyone
-The illusion of a gambling system when it is voluntary socialized medicine that cuts costs by refusing to pay for some people
-the absurdity of expecting people to keep insurance from working when the insurance purpose is to pay for care for conditions that make is difficult or impossible to work
-the scam of underpaid working poor people not being able to afford healthcare or anything else because their companies do not pay fair wages much less share profit
-the scam of insurance being called a "benefit" when many employees pay for it themselves every month
-companies paying people in benefits instead of wages in the first place
-broken contract behavior from the government who promises health care and then takes it back
-senators making salaries for life instead of just when they are working and then making all their decisions to "save taxpayer money"
-abuse and exploitation from employers who know their workers are not free to leave jobs because of dependency on insurance

People have been patient with this outrageous scam that has cost our country freedom and lives for many years. Obamacare was a good start to fix it. Bad laws and bad people have exhausted my patience and strength as a libertarian worker and I think I will probably advocate for single payer Medicare for all. People will call me a commie but I think it is a solution that could set people free to be prosperous and the whole deficit could disappear almost instantly when people use their gifts to be productive instead of panicking to keep insurance while companies squeeze the life out of everyone.

More of a free market option could be a competitive system where everyone has individual insurance and it is like car insurance. This could also solve the pro-life pro-choice disagreements because people could choose companies that cover or dont cover certain costs. But really this option is probably what should have happened twenty years ago and people instead chose to let the insurance companies and employers take advantage of everyone.

Social Justice was my religion in fourth grade

Hmmm, which is better... trickle down economics from the corporations or trickle down guilt manipulation from the social work schools. I just don't know... but people who call every single good thing in life "privilege" are no allies of mine.

The Cutting of The Cake makers

Hi, would people like to hear my opinion about gay wedding cakes? Some people think it is a no brainer like refusing to make a certain kind of cake for certain people is automatically discrimination, but I do not really think so. I would kill myself if people forced me to create something that I did not want to create. I think that the rule should be that anyone should be allowed to buy any cake that a cake maker makes, but that cake makers should only have to make original cakes according to designs they choose and believe in themselves. So if they have wedding cakes and gay people want one for a wedding, they should have to sell it, but if some loser comes in their shop and demands that they design some nasty cake or some cake with icing saying something they don't believe in then they have no moral obligation whatsoever to comply and should also not have any kind of legal obligation. So to me it is about design. I know that some people think that their religious rights are violated if they have to sell a cake to someone that they don't want to, but to me, especially since gay marriage is legal, then it is reasonable to expect them to treat everyone the same.

I think that part of this has to do with how personal a cake is or isn't. You are not the officiating minister because you made someone a cake. The cake doesn't have that kind of meaning, and if it did, then wouldn't your cake sale be the wedding? Everyone knows that it is not.

So now people are like oh, funny you should mention ministers. They are next on our list of people we want to persecute. Well hmm I guess that is part of gay marriage tradition now isn't it? People choose the flowers they want, and choose their wedding party, and then choose the religious people whose lives they want to ruin.

Daily Grime

I remember as a kid having so many hilarious laughs with middle school and high school friends whenever we would say "What if someone did such and such," and it would be some inappropriate thing that we all knew was absurd. And everyone had a basic understanding of societal norms, and how terrible it would be to see some kind of embarrassing commercial when you were with your grandmother, or how wrong it would be for a teacher to do something crazy like show pornography in class. I think that these standards in our minds became the foundation for some deep appreciation of hilarious jokes, some of which were homemade, and some of which were expertly presented in movies and on TV.

But now, as if someone went and dumped all the spices ever made into everyone's food and drinks and even ice cream, we have nasty images and nasty jokes and nasty music in our faces and minds constantly everywhere we turn. People can say that is not true but I do not believe them. If you need to make some copies at an office store, you will get it done while listening to a top 40 song that is more explicit than a medical anatomy class and has people making actual sexual noises. Bus drivers who wanted decent, honest work, suddenly find themselves driving down the road with huge underwear ads featuring completely naked people on their bus for everyone to see. I really can't think of anything more disrespectful to a community and especially to a worker doing their job. How disgusting. If you say anything about it, you are considered a prude, but I think that most people, and possibly everyone, knows in their hearts that our culture has a problem and it probably is contributing to high rates of abuse, and isn't that far from abuse itself. Some people get no break from it and do not even know what it is like to think about other things and play regular games and care about a normal movie storyline or hear a song that isn't some nasty metaphor, or even that is a metaphor instead of being a base and crude description of bodily functions. There used to be such a thing as a dirty joke, because some jokes weren't dirty. Now the people behind and in front of the media are the dirty jokes who have ruined our society. When I speak out about it or even frown, people literally turn up the music louder to humiliate me, but I will still make my case for a Muzak revolution, not because it is my job to clean all the rapists' minds, but because I know that things were funnier and life was zippier when dirt had its place, and that place wasn't everywhere.

People At Half Mast

I have taken a break from mad blog posts and it could be because I have recovered from people hurting me and my general anger has decreased. I think my non-madblog posts are better, and I am tempted to just say nevermind about this blog. But it is a good place for opinions, and I think I will share a thought about the flag protests, which I do think are warranted. Trump didn't just express his opinion that flag protestors should be fired, but in my opinion actually tried to influence NFL bosses to fire their players. So yeah, people should protest. And other people's knee-jerk objection to their very appropriate protest exposes another problem which is the intellectual laziness that has resulted in a lot of our political problems. For years, people have just let themselves believe that the soldiers are the only true American heroes, and that people like workers or taxpayers or even children don't also contribute to our society in heroic ways, and that the flag doesn't and shouldn't also represent them. So if someone suggests that there may be some problems represented by that flag, people automatically say that the wounded veterans are the ones being disrespected. But really, the protestors are defending the true value that the flag should have represented, and in that way are supporting the veterans by trying to insure that their sacrifice is not in vain.

A lot has already been said about all of this, but I did feel like sharing this opinion, because I have always been aware as a low paid retail worker that some people's contributions to our society are celebrated and some people don't even earn a living wage while their companies rake in millions of dollars of profit from their labor, which then goes to pay the salaries of people who are declared heroes as soon as they sign up for service. But there are a lot of heroes, and sports stars who have overcome great odds do stand for something too and are right to protect everyone when some loser threatens to take away everything they have earned.

Trials and Errors

Well everyone, it is a Thursday morning in October and I am starting my day mad at Pope Francis. It is not really anything personal except he told everyone that the death penalty is wrong and contrary to the gospel and Christianity. I think he is the one who is wrong this time, not the death penalty, and people who do what they are supposed to and are morally secure have no problem sending murderers, child abusers, and rapists onward to Judgement Day for God to decide what is next for them. And one of those reasons is that there might not be a bad enough punishment possible for them on earth. As much as people want to seem compassionate by saying it is no one's right to take another life, the fact is that the humane thing to do is to rid our streets of rapists and murderers and to trust that there can be more justice and mercy beyond this world. So really the thing that is not Christian is thinking that all we see is all there is and everything is up to us in such a way that we have to be too careful to do what is right and err on the side of letting traffickers and heroin dealers ruin everyone's lives. There are horrible things happening in our country, and I think the real question before us these days is not whether the death penalty is moral, but whether the murderers and rapists should still get a trial beforehand.

The Worst Policies

Sometimes I wonder what kind of jokes comedians are making and have been saying for the past twenty years because to me sometimes it seems like nothing is funny. It just seems like this whole country and world is a tragedy.

I mean are they making jokes about how Subway's mayonnaise isn't really mayonnaise? Because I looked it up online after tasting a horrible mysterious white plastic-like goop and sure enough, there are no eggs in the "recipe," or should I say "chemical formula." And at the store in my neighborhood, if you say you want Cheddar Cheese, they give you a shredded mix that has a few specks of cheddar and they don't even say anything like "We don't have Cheddar, we have this little mysterious mix that we know isn't what you want or what you asked for." And hmm I mean I hope the turkey is turkey but we don't really know anymore, do we?

And then okay, maybe it is just the fast food industry, except that iphones seem engineered to be a disposable product now because the charging ports wear out in a year ever since Apple started using the chargers that have that tiny little port instead of the wider port that was more dependable. And when I try to access my library of music there is this other button that tries to get you to sign up for their apple music program. And then it is hard to access my old library of music in the first place, so I think, hmm, do I have to rebuy music? I know I am not the only one. I've heard many rumors that Apple tries to make their products become obsolete fast on purpose, but is "obsolete" really the same as "defective?" I don' t think it is, honestly.

That was funny when I said the word "honestly," wasn't it.

Noise Levels

Well everyone, today I called my favorite restaurant to ask them if they play their music from a playlist and the guy told me that people play music from their Ipods and they have a jukebox. I told him the reason I was wondering was because last night when I was one of just a few customers there, the music started off great and then turned into the song "I wanna sex you up," and I suspected deliberate harassment. The manager was not happy to hear a legal word like that but really I am doing him a favor because they could get sued for stuff like that even though people who do that stuff think that people don't realize that they are humiliating people on purpose. But some of us do know because we get treated that way all the time. I don't think that case is as clear as when I was in a junk and antique store in Brooklyn and I was the only customer and there was just one piece-of-garbage male employee who immediately put in a C.D. that started with the song "I just want to m. l. to you." Oh, it's a classic alright, and as mad as I was, I didn't realize until later that what it really is is classic sexual harassment. Another store in my neighborhood cranked up some nasty music past 100 decibels one day when I walked in but I stayed and bought some shoes and the store people were just young teens or twenty-somethings who I suspected had experienced more racism even than the blatant racial and sexual harassment they were treating me with right then so I did not even call their corporate office to complain. But it is interesting to me that all these people think their offense and the deliberate nature of it is undetectable, because really it is pretty obvious, even amid all the offensive canned playlists from corporate offices that are meant to speed up their store traffic or build a brand that is officially too cool for people with morals or decency. In the end, people will say it is free speech, but I don't think that's what they would so quickly defend if they heard me say my free speech that I usually say in those situations, which is "Death and Shame to you In The Name of Jesus Christ." I am sad, because all I really wanted was peace of mind, or in some cases, to have nice background music, which is also what I would rather hear than the agonized shrieking and wailing that all of humanity will hear and rejoice over when all those people and other rapists like them are burning in hell some day in a future that actually isn't that far away.

Taking Down the Statutes

For today's mad blog post I would like to say that I think almost all statute of limitations laws that keep people from bringing abuse charges after a certain amount of time has passed are a terrible injustice and an embarrassment to our society and all of so called "civilization." These kinds of laws do one thing, which is to help bad people get away with child abuse and other violations. The endorsement of this behavior through law actually to me should make people really wonder if there can be such thing as good people in power. I have always believed that there can be and must be, but laws like this are suspicious. What are people hiding and getting away with to maintain their control? It must be something awful if there are laws saying that people's accusations don't count once they have found the strength to report what has really happened.

Monopoly

No need to make too big a deal of it, but this week, the cable company charged me five dollars just to let me pay my own bill for internet service. And I was also thinking about how I rent my modem from them and may be paying ten times what the modem is worth because of that, which is absurd, though if I were stronger I could have bought a different modem. But I think that is the idea, and it is interesting to think about with apartment rent gouging, too. If our system suddenly became a rent to own system where your past rent was credited to you as going toward the cost of a place to live, I think people would freak out and talk about communism. And yet with the modem situation, the absurdity of people paying more than something is worth and still not owning it is easily apparent.

An Eternal Harvest of Love:
American Literature Final Exams
by Refried Bean

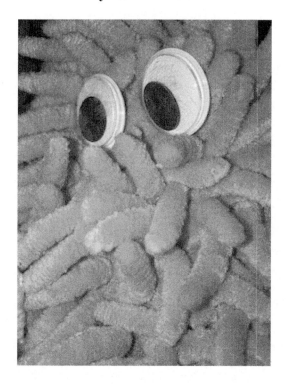

In this section of the book, I am including copies of two English tests that I created when I taught 9th and 11th grade English for one year. The first test is the final exam for my 1st semester American Literature class of eleventh graders, and the second test is an improved final exam for the last semester. That last test has about two hundred questions. I think the last few questions could be different from what I actually used, but this was the copy in my computer and it is almost exactly the same.

I think some people might have fun trying to see if they know the answers to the tests, but I mainly am sharing it because it is an interesting part of my life that I feel like writing about just a little bit. I got in trouble for the first semester exam, which had a lot of joke questions and the answer to every single one was "C." I wrote the exam at the last minute after spending part of Christmas break in the mental hospital. The hospitalization was a precaution because of some mania from my mental illness that was triggered from a few tough days cashiering at the Barnes and Noble where I worked part-time during my first year of teaching.

It turned out to be my only year of teaching. In the beginning, I was reluctant to take the job because I had decided that I was too scared to teach and wanted to be an advertising copywriter after all, but my parents said that really I needed to go ahead and teach since I had just done a Masters program in teaching English. So I did, and I was so scared, but within just a few weeks I really liked it, and by the end I loved it and wanted to stay and keep teaching as a career. But I did get in trouble for the joke exam, which you will see isn't that funny or rude, and I guess there were other things that the school thought I did not do well enough. Really I taught three different classes each semester, and the classes were all an hour and half long, which is pretty crazy. That is a lot of preparation and planning and speaking, and I really think I only had about five or ten minutes of "dead air" the whole year. We did a lot of creative writing in my classes, and I tried to work on grammar and read stories in the class time so it was not always some kind of reading check instead of learning time.

I think I did pretty good, and I was heartbroken when my contract was not renewed. But that year of teaching was also when some of my mental illness symptoms got worse. During the school year, I thought that people were putting songs on the radio that called me a hypocrit, and saying things were hot or cold to let me know if my behavior was good, and putting secret messages in conversations to criticize me and publicly humiliate me. I did a couple of times ask for a little reality check from people, like when I asked a janitor if the mop machine smelled like gasoline because I had done something bad. It is possible that these few cracks and breaks in my effort to stay okay might have influenced the school's decision that I was not the teacher they wanted. But it did confuse me, because even with the feelings of shame and persecution, I did think I did a good job preparing each day and leading class discussions about great literature that I sometimes chose myself. I finished the year thinking that I might be one of the 8000 best first year teachers that ever lived. Since then I have thought that maybe I was wrong about being that great, because a lot of teachers are pretty awesome, but I do think I did a good job. And despite my disorganization, I managed my classroom mostly with kindness and rapport instead of rules and referrals, and I do think that caring is part of education.

1) Why did Hester Prynne have to wear a red A on her chest in <u>The Scarlet Letter</u>?
    a. she was a die hard <u>Twilight</u> fan
    b. she was an A student
    c. her community wanted to ostracize her for committing adultery
    d. she wanted to star in a novel

2) What did the A on Hester Prynne's chest stand for?
    a. apples
    b. abstinence
    c. adultery
    d. alcoholic
    e. Atlas Shrugged
    f. ridiculosity
    g. angels
    h. aspirin

3) A story that is passed down through generations and explains why the world is the way it is is called what?
    a. parody
    b. novel
    c. myth
    d. a cartoon

4) In "Sinners in the Hands of an Angry God", Jonathan Edwards suggests that many people are being held over a gaping fire pit by
    a. Satan's minions
    b. a monster's hand
    c. a single thread because of God's mercy
    d. a bulldozer from the cartoon "Bob the Builder"

5) At the end of "Sinners in the Hands of An Angry God," Jonathan Edwards reassures his congregation that they may be saved from the fire

a) by doing their best in Ms. Efird's American Lit class

b) by learning their multiplication tables

c) by accepting God's forgiveness offered through Jesus's death on the cross.

d) by making sure that their high school football team is ranked number one in the nation.

6) In "The Yellow Wallpaper", what is the author's opinion about doctors?

a. that they are helpful

b. they usually pay attention to their patients

c. they gave bad advice about depression because they didn't understand it.

d. they should only work in hospitals

e. they don't believe in depression as an illness

7) What color was the wallpaper in "The Yellow Wallpaper"?

a. red

b. blue

c. yellow

d. green

(y'all can thank "student's name" for this question)

8) Who taught a chicken to walk backwards?

a. student's name

b.student's name

c. Flannery O'Connor

d. Nathaniel Hawthorne

9) How did Sam Clemens get the pen name "Mark Twain?"
   a. it was a nickname from fourth grade
   b. his mommy gave it to him
   c. either from a bar tab or because that's how they measured the water on river boats
   d. Ms. Efird just made it up.

10) What was one of Mark Twain's occupations besides being an author?
   a. slave owner
   b. dog catcher
   c. river boat captain
   d. clown

11) In The Adventures of Huckleberry Finn, who helps Huck and is helped by him on his journey?
   a. Pap
   b. his fairy god mother
   c. Jim
   d. Aunt Polly
   e. The Duke and Dauphin

In The Adventures of Huckleberry Finn, the duke and dauphin are
   a. Heroic and noble
   b. Shakespearian scholars
   c. Con men who take advantage of people
   d. True royalty

13) How is the south depicted in The Adventures of Huckleberry Finn?
   a. Rich
   b. Smart and polite
   c. Ignorant and full of hypocrisy
   d. Sophisticated

14) Which of the following is not an example of irony in <u>Huck Finn?</u>
    a. The fact that Huck is more Christlike than the official Christians in the novel
    b. The fact that Jim is so wise despite being regarded as ignorant
    c. All of these
    d. The fact that Huck is so honest about telling a story in which he is constantly dishonest
    e. The fact that Ms. Efird discussed hypocrisy on a day when she had only skimmed the chapters that were assigned
    f. The fact that the only healthy family in the book was separated

15) All of the following were satirized in <u>Huck Finn</u> except
    a. the literary movement called Romanticism
    b.the southern Christians
    c. realism
    d. race relations in the South
    e. family life in the South

16)Huckleberry Finn's dad was
    a. Pap
    b. Drunk all the time
    c. All of these answers
    d. Racist
    e. Opposed to Huck being educated

17) Three types of irony are
    a. Ironic, ironical, ironocentric
    b. Ironicatious, ironirific, irontastic
    c. Verbal, situational, and dramatic
    d. Ironifierous, ironicatating, ironolicious

18) A rhetorical question
   a. Is a question that starts with the word "Who"
   b. Is a question you ask to a child
   c. Is a question you ask to make a point and not because you really want an answer
   d. Is a multiple choice question

19) In John Cheever's "Enormous Radio", what did the radio do?
   a. Glowed with an eerie green light
   b. Played jazz all the time
   c. Allowed the Wescotts to eavesdrop on everyone in the apartment
   d. Tuned in only to country stations

20) What was Wall-E's best friend?
   a. A rubic's cube
   b. A tree
   c. A cockroach
   d. E.T.

21) Emily Dickinson was
   a. A poet from New England
   b. Someone who struggled with her faith in God
   c. A,b, and d
   d. A recluse who wrote hundreds and hundreds of poems with little recognition until after she died.

22) How did Ernest Hemingway die?
   a. He was killed by Emily Grierson in "A Rose for Emily".
   b. Dorothy Parker made him die laughing
   c. He shot himself in the head in 1961 after suffering from depression.
   d. He put his head in an oven

23) When is it okay to kill yourself?
    a. When you are Ernest Hemingway
    b. When you are Sylvia Plath
    c. Never. Stay alive no matter what.
    d. When you are severely depressed

24) In Sylvia Plath's poem, "Mushrooms," the mushrooms represent
    a. Superstar famous people
    b. Famous politicians
    c. Humble, meek people who are often overlooked and "stepped on"
    d. Monster robots who want to hurt high school students

25) The short story "Minority Report"
    a. is about an enormous radio
    b. is about a machine called the multivac
    c. is about a concept called "Pre-crime"
    d. is an example of historical fiction

26) Flannery O'Connor
    a. was Irish
    b. was a Yankee
    c. was a devout Catholic whose stories featured "Grotesques"
    d. wrote about a boy and a slave traveling down the Mississippi River

27) A sentence with two independent clauses is called
    a. simple
    b. complex
    c. compound
    d. a life sentence

28) This southern author was famous for his "Stream of consciousness" writing:
   a. Isaac Asimov
   b. Ayn Rand
   c. William Faulkner
   d. student's name

29) "I like cheese." is a
   a. complex sentence
   b. a compound sentence
   c. a simple sentence
   d. a question

30) Who taught a chicken to walk backwards?
   a. student's name
   b. student's name
   c. Flannery O'Connor
   d. student's name

31) When did the Harlem Renaissance take place?
   a. the 1400s
   b. the 1950s
   c. the 1920s
   d. Ms. Efird actually made the whole thing up. There was no Harlem renaissance.

32) What is Robert Frost's poem, "Birches" about?
   a. monkeys playing on a tree
   b. people and their best friends
   c. kids swinging on trees
   d. people going on a haunted trail

33) What was the classroom goldfish's name?
   a. Goldy
   b. Hemingway
   c. he died tragically before he got a name
   d. Slurpy

34) Why did Ms. Efird let Slurpy go in a lake?
   a. because she couldn't keep the tank clean
   b. because she wanted to feed the other fish there
   c. because Slurpy had a hundred little babies and she didn't know what else to do
   d. because Slurpy had been a bad suckerfish

35) In "The Life You Save May Be Your Own", Mr. Shiftlet left Lucynell at
   a. a hotel
   b. a church
   c. a diner
   d. a house

36) Zora Neale Hurston is famous for
   a. compiling slave folk tales and preserving the dialect
   b. writing insightful essays about race relations
   c. all of these
   d. writing a novel called Their Eyes Were Watching God

37) Robert Frost often related deeper meaning and understanding about life to
   a. women
   b. apples
   c. nature
   d. a raisin in the sun

38) What happens to a dream deferred?
   a. does it dry up like a raisin in the sun?
   b. or fester like a sore and then run?
   c. all of these
   d. Does it stink like rotten meat?
   e. Or crust and sugar over—like a syrupy sweet?
   f. maybe it just sags like a heavy load
   g. Or does it explode?

39) This author married his cousin, but she died of tuberculosis, just like all the other women in his life, and he was depressed all the time and wrote horror stories.
   a. Emily Dickinson
   b. Anne Tyler
   c. Edgar Allen Poe
   d. teacher's name

40) When Anne Bradstreet's house burned down, she
   a. went around burning other houses down
   b. started the Salem witch trials
   c. got over it, declared that her treasure was in heaven, and then wrote a unch of poems to torture Byrnes students
   d. decided to wear a scarlet letter

41) Martin Luther King believed that
   a. mistreated black people should gain their rights by any means necessary
   b. mistreated black people should just turn the other cheek and allow things to remain the same
   c. misreated black people should practice nonviolent resistance (civil disobedience)
   d. mistreated black people should paint themselves purple.

42) In sentences, noun clauses can function as
   a. adverbial clauses
   b. verbs
   c. subjects, direct objects, predicate nominatives, and objects of prepositions
   d. punctuation

43) "Give me liberty or give me death" is from a famous speech by
   a. Benjamin Franklin
   b. Oprah Winfrey
   c. Patrick Henry
   d. John Adams

44) When a piece of writing only tells one side of a story, it is
   a. too bad
   b. refiberative
   c. biased
   d. objective

45) Creation stories from around the world often include
   a. ideas about spaceships
   b. bibliographies
   c. similar elements, such as twins, a huge flood, evil and good, and a tree
   d.quotes from Herman Melville

46) in a story, a character who changes is called
   a. flat
   b. round
   c. dynamic
   d. rebuffatory

50) This author dropped out of high school
   a. Isaac Asimov
   b. Sylvia Plath
   c. William Faulkner
   d. Robert Frost

Essay Question (choose one) (you answer should be one page long)Make sure your answer has a thesis and three supporting arguments.

What is a recurring theme in American Literature and how do different authors approach that topic?

Which author made the greatest contribution to American Literature and why?

If the literature book could only have three selections in it, which three should they be and why?

Extra Credit:
What would you change about this class?
What would you not change about his class?
Write down anything else you know about American Literature that I didn't ask about on the test:

Here is the improved final exam.

1) A fictional story that explains the origin of the universe is called a
  a. Trickster tale
  b. Creation myth
  c. Parable
  d. Darwinian bang
2) The central problem in a story, usually between two opposing forces, is called
  a. Theme
  b. Plot
  c. Conflict
  d. Resolution
3) An extended metaphor is
  a. A comparison using like or as
  b. A comparison that is developed and continued throughout a work of literature
  c. A comparison of two opposite characters
  d. A comparison of two or more literary movements
4) Internal conflict can be expressed as
  a. Man vs. himself
  b. Man vs. man
  c. Man vs. nature
  d. All of the above
5) Man vs. nature is an example of
  a. Indirect characterization
  b. Direct characterization
  c. internal conflict
  d. external conflict
6) Specific descriptions that appeal to a person's sense of smell, taste, touch, sight, or hearing are called
  a. Sensory images
  b. Sensory details
  c. Sensational themes
  d. Sensitive content

7) A primary source is a
   a. Book
   b. First-hand account
   c. Piece of hearsay
   d. Novel
8) An epitaph is
   a. A gravestone slogan
   b. A poem about death
   c. A speech you give at someone's funeral
   d. A paragraph that rambles
9) Metered poetry that sounds like five heartbeats is
   a. Iambic pentameter
   b. Trochaic triameter
   c. Anapestic pentameter
   d. Iambic octameter
10) All of the following are often used to emphasize ideas in poetry except
   a. Meter
   b. Rhyme
   c. Repitition
   d. prose
11) An allusion is
   a. A reference to a familiar work of art or literature
   b. A choice that a main character makes in a story
   c. The main idea of a story
   d. The settling of conflict
12) A question that accuses is a
   a. Rhetorical question
   b. Loaded question
   c. Concise question
   d. Faulty cause question
13) A question that someone asks without expecting an answer is
   a. A rhetorical question
   b. A loaded question
   c. A concise question
   d. A faulty cause question

14) Situational Irony is
   a. When a situtation is the opposite of what you would expect
   b. Sarcasm
   c. When the audience knows something that a character doesn't
   d. An unresolved ending
15) Verbal Irony is
   a. When a situation is the opposite of what you would expect
   b. Sarcasm
   c. When the audience knows something that a character doesn't
   d. An unresolved ending
16) Dramatic Irony is
   a. When a situation is the opposite of what you would expect
   b. Sarcasm
   c. When the audience knows something that a character doesn't know
   d. An unresolved ending
17) satire is
   a. a collection of puns
   b. narrative poetry
   c. humor that criticizes
   d. fables that teach

18) A character who is the opposite of another character in a story is called a
   a. Double
   b. A round character
   c. A flat character
   d. A foil
19) A dynamic character is a character who
   a. Stays the same in a story
   b. Changes throughout a story
   c. Has multiple characteristics
   d. Has just one or two traits

20) A round character is a character who
    a. Stays the same in a story
    b. Changes throughout a story
    c. Has multiple characteristics
    d. Has just one or two traits
21) If an article only tells one side of the story, it is
    a. Objective
    b. Biased
    c. Confirmed
    d. extended
22) A concession is
    a. An acknowledgement of an opposing viewpoint in a persuasive speech or paper
    b. A refusal to see another side of an argument
    c. a term for changing one's mind
    d. a thesis
23) A concept or idea in a story that anyone can relate to is called a
    a. Conflict
    b. Central problem
    c. Universal theme
    d. Plot
24) If something is objective, it is
    a. One-sided
    b. From one perspective
    c. Factual and accurate
    d. From a primary source
25) Taking credit for someone else's work or copying is called
    a. Plagiarism
    b. MLA format
    c. Citation
    d. Parenthetical documentation

26) In a research paper or essay, the statement of the main idea is also called a
   a. Conclusion
   b. Thesis
   c. Works cited page
   d. concession
27) Alliteration is
   a. The repetition of consonant sounds
   b. The repitition of vowel sounds
   c. The repetition of rhyme
   d. The repetition of meter
28) Giving a nonhuman thing human characteristics is called
   a. Simile
   b. Metonomy
   c. Personification
   d. Imagery
29) Meter is
   a. A poem's rhyme scheme
   b. A poem's word count
   c. Song lyrics
   d. A poem's rhythm
30) When a poet makes lines almost rhyme, it is called
   a. Slant rhyme
   b. Rhyme scheme
   c. Consonation
   d. Alliteration
31) A word's connotation is
   a. Its dictionary definition
   b. Its symbolic meaning
   c. its etymology
   d. its positive or negative associations
32) A word's denotation is
   a. Its dictionary definition
   b. Its symbolic meaning
   c. its etymology
i   d. ts positive or negative associations

33) If an author uses direct characterization, he
   a. Lets the reader guess what his character is like
   b. Gives subtle clues about his characters
   c. Flat out tells the reader what the character is like
   d. Makes the character change throughout the story
34) A symbol
   a. Is an object or person that represents something else
   b. Is always an object
   c. Is always visual
   d. None of the above
35) Writing in a rambling style that imitates the free thought in someone's mind is called
   a. Minimalism
   b. Realism
   c. Stream of consciousness
   d. Iambic pentameter
36) A funeral poem is an
   a. Eulogy
   b. Epitaph
   c. Equifax
   d. Elegy
37) The emotional feel of a story is its
   a. Mood
   b. Theme
   c. Plot
   d. Connotation
38) The author's attitude in a piece of literature is called
   a.Theme
   b. Tone
   c. Plot
   d. Frame
39) The Puritans
   a. were settlers from England
   b. came to America in the 1400s.
   c. believed in many gods
   d. wore many bright colors

40) The Puritans

    a. believed that God has already decided who will go to heaven and who will go to hell

    b. believed that God would never punish anyone for their sins

    c. believed that witchcraft was okay as long as you did it outside the village

    d. believed that people should not get married

41)　The Puritans

    a. started Harvard University

    b. sometimes alienated people who differed in beliefs or lifestyle

    c. made great contributions to American Literature

    d. settled mainly in New England.

42)　Hester's scarlet letter was an

    a. A for adultery

    b. A for assumption

    c. A for affair

    d. A for Agony

43.　In The Scarlet Letter, Dimmesdale is

    a. a minster

    b. Pearl's father

    c. "taken care of" by Chillingworth

    d. tormented by guilt

    e. all of the above

44.　In The Scarlet Letter, Hester is

    a. married to Chillingworth

    b. married to Dimmesdale

    c. hated by everyone until she dies

    d. all of the above

    e. none of the above

45.　Hester Prynne is the subject of

    a. controversy

    b. gossip

    c. admiration

    d. the novel

    e. all of the above

46. The Scarlet Letter was written by
   a. Nathaniel Hawthorne
   b. Anne Bradstreet
   c. Jonathan Edwards
   d. Arthur Miller
47. During the Salem Witch Trials
   a. witches finally got what they deserved
   b. Puritans falsely accused many people and put them to death
   c. many people died of tuberculosis
   d. Edgar Allan Poe started writing

48. In "Sinners in the Hands of An Angry God," Jonathan Edwards reassures listeners that
   a. Jesus died for our sins and God will welcome us back
   b. Hell is not real
   c. The Bible's description of Hell was distorted by translation
   d. the thread that holds us over hell is very strong
49. The poet who stayed at home as a recluse and wrote over 1775 poems was
   a. Walt Whitman
   b. Robert Frost
   c. Emily Dickinson
   d. Billy Collins
50. The poet who lived on a farm for a while and wrote nature poems was
   a. Walt Whitman
   b. Robert Frost
   c. Emily Dickinson
   d. Billy Collins
51. The poet who made free verse popular was
   a. Walt Whitman
   b. Robert Frost
   c. Emily Dickinson
   d. Billy Collins

52. Emily Dickinson's poems were
   a. long ballads
   b. mostly sonnets
   c. limericks
   d. short poems with dashes and occasional rhyme

53. This author was famous for his "Stream of consciousness" writing.
   a. Isaac Asimov
   b. William Faulkner
   c. Philip K. Dick
   d. John Cheever

54. Flannery O'Connor
   a. was a Protestant Christian who opposed most Catholic doctrine.
   b. included a lot of violence in her stories because she was not a Christian.
   c. was a devout Catholic who created many fundamentalist Protestant Christian characters in her stories.
   d. avoided religious themes in her stories because it is so controversial.

55. This author wrote a book in every single one of the Dewey Decimal System categories except philosophy
   a. John Updike
   b Flannery O'Connor
   c. Isaac Asimov
   d. Charlotte Perkins Gilman

56. Charlotte Perkins Gilman wrote "The Yellow Wallpaper"
   a. in protest to poor medical treatment she received during a period of depression
   b. to help herself deal with the disappointment of not having a thriving interior design business
   c. to urge schizophrenics to work together in fundraising efforts for people suffering from mental illness
   d. to encourage women to be more domestic and avoid men's activities like writing and medicine.

57.   This author, whose father died of lupus, also developed the disease and died young.
    a. Isaac Asimov
    b. John Updike
    c. Flannery O'Connor
    d. William Faulkner

58. This author was from Mississippi and wrote mostly about the people in that area.
    a. John Updike
    b. William Faulkner
    c. Charlotte Perkins Gilman
    d. Isaac Asimov

59. In "The life You Save May Be Your Own," Mr. Shiftlet picks up the hitchhiker because he
    a. is a benevolent Christian man who makes time for anyone in need.
    b. feels guilty about leaving Lucynell in the diner.
    c. wants to help the kid turn out better than him
    d. is hoping the hitchhiker has some cash.
    e. doesn't know how to get to Mobile.

60. The oncoming storm in "The Life You Save May Be Your Own" represents
    a. God's judgement
    b. human pride
    c. sin and redemption
    d. mental handicap

61.   In "A Rose For Emily," the town discovers that
    a. Emily poisoned Homer and slept with his dead body for years.
    b. Emily had an affair with the black man who worked for her.
    c. their gossip was unjustified and insensitive.
    d. the taxation of the city was extreme because of Emily's relationship with the mayor.

62. A "grotesque" is a type of character found in
   a. pulp fiction
   b. Flannery O'Connor stories
   c. Wal-Mart at 3 am.
   d. John Cheever stories
   e. "The Yellow Wallpaper."
63. Isaac Asimov
   a. was a practicing Jewish believer.
   b. refused to be canonized as a Catholic saint despite mass efforts to recognize him as such.
   c. was an atheist
   d. spent time as a missionary in France

64. In "The Yellow Wallpaper," the doctor
   a. is condescending to his wife
   b. dismisses her symptoms as being insignificant
   c. takes her to a large house to get some rest
   d. suggests that she lay in bed all day instead of writing
   e. all of the above
65. In "The Yellow Wallpaper"
   a. a woman becomes trapped inside the ugly wallpaper
   b. a woman begins having delusions while trapped in a room with wallpaper she doesn't like.
   c. a woman overcomes over whelming obstacles to become a renowned psychiatrist
   d. a woman becomes sick because of asbestos and mold in the wallpaper.
66. A story that is tragiocomic
   a. includes elements that are simultaneously funny and sad.
   b. includes elements that are sad and then switches to sheer hilarity.
   c. starts off funny but has a sad ending
   d. always includes the death of a main character.

67. This author taught a chicken to walk backwards:
    a. Flannery O'Connor
    b. John Cheever
    c. Charlotte Perkins Gilman
    d. principal's name
68. Edgar Alan Poe may have modeled the plague in "The Masque of The Red Death" after this disease, which killed many of the women he loved.
    a. The Black Plague
    b. The Flu Epidemic
    c. Tuberculosis
    d. AIDS
    e. Cholera
69. Edgar Alan Poe invented the
    a. cotton gin
    b. detective story
    c. short story
    d. limerick
    e. surprise ending
70. In "A Rose For Emily," the town discovers that
    a. Emily poisoned Homer and slept with his dead body for years.
    b. Emily had an affair with her yard man.
    c. their gossip was unjustified and insensitive.
    d. the taxation of the city was extreme because of Emily's relationship with the mayor.
71. The colors of the last room in "Masque of The Red Death" are
    a. purple and white
    b. red and black
    c. grey and white
    d. blue and grey
72. In "A Worn Path", the worn path is a metaphor representing any
    a. journey to freedom
    b. "habit of love"
    c. "reconciliation of family"
    d. one-time heroic sacrifice

73. In "A Worn Path," it is ironic that the nurse uses the word "Charity" because
    a. Charity was Phoenix Jackson's maiden name.
    b. Charity's grandson didn't need it.
    c. Charity means "hope"
    d. Phoenix is the one demonstrating true charity.

74. In "A Worn Path", it is ironic that the hunter says Phoenix is going to see Santa because
    a. Santa is not real
    b. Phoenix is the real Santa of the story
    c. the hunter just came back from seeing Santa
    d. Phoenix prayed to the real St. Nicholas

75. Martin Luther King believed that
    a. anyone oppressed should gain their rights by any means necessary
    b. anyone oppressed should just turn the other cheek and allow things to remain the same
    c. anyone oppressed should practice nonviolent resistance (civil disobedience)
    d. anyone oppressed should wait for someone else to do something about it.

76. Malcolm X defended his violent ways by
    a. comparing himself to the founding fathers
    b. saying that the unprotected must protect themselves by any means necessary
    c. Disagreeing with Martin Luther King Jr.
    d. all of the above

77. Martin Luther King Jr said that the three possible reactions to oppression are
    a. fighting as a group, fighting individually, and fighting in pairs
    b. fighting back, giving in, or nonviolent resistance
    c. uncivil disobedience, rejection of authority, and war
    d. all of the above

78. Martin Luther King's Civil Rights approach can be called
   a. nonviolent resistance
   b. any means necessary
   c. passivity
   d. nonviolent compliance
79. Huckleberry Finn lives where at the beginning of the novel?
   a. In Cairo
   b. On a raft
   c. With Pap
   d. With the Widow Douglass
80. Why does Jim run away from Miss Watson?
   a. she treats him harshly
   b. He was tired of living in captivity
   c. she was going to sell him and separate him from his family
   d. he wanted to become rich.
81. In The Adventures of Huckleberry Finn, Mark Twain criticizes racism, religion in the south, slavery, and what other two things?
   a. government and economics
   b. women and children
   c. corporate greed and welfare
   d. education and the American family
82. In The Adventures of Huckleberry Finn, Realism and Romanticism are embodied by
   a. Tom and Huck
   b. Huck and Jim
   c. Jim and Pap
   d. The Widow Douglas and Miss Watson
83. On their journey, Huck and Jim become
   a. close to nature
   b. close to each other
   c. close to getting killed
   d. all of the above
   e. none of the above

84. The way Huck wrestles with whether or not to help Jim is an example of
   a. external conflict
   b. internal conflict
   c. direct characterization
   d. indirect characterization
85. A conflict in Huck Finn is
   a. man vs. man
   b. man vs. nature
   c. man vs. society
   d. man vs. himself
   e. all of the above
86. Huck Finn changes in the novel by
   a. growing up
   b. taking more responsibility
   c. following his heart instead of giving in to societal pressure
   d. all of the above
87. In Huck Finn, the Duke and Dauphin are
   a. admirable role models
   b. con men
   c. murderers
   d. father figures
88. Jim's foil is
   a. Huck
   b. Miss Watson
   c. The Widow Douglas
   d. Pap
89. Mark Twain got his nickname from working as
   a. a bartender
   b. a steamboat captain
   c. a teacher
   d. a farmer

90. Mark Twain criticized southern hypocrisy by
    a. making Miss Watson sell Jim
    b. having Huck Finn interpret the Bible literally
    c. exposing the injustice of slavery
    d. all of the above.
91. Huck is more like Jesus than the Christians in the book because
    a. he never lies
    b. he is willing to go to hell for someone
    c. he helps to build an orphanage
    d. he reads his Bible daily
92. The Harlem Renaissance poet who wrote a collection of poems based on the sermons of black preachers is
    a. Langston Hughes
    b. Countee Cullen
    c. James Weldon Johnson
    d. Robert Frost
93. The Harlem Renaissance took place during the
    a. 1890s
    b. 1920s
    c. 1950s
    d. 1990s
94. Harlem is a neighborhood in
    a. New York
    b. New Jersey
    c. Duncan
    d. Lyman
95. True or False: All literature from the Harlem Renaissance was about race,
    a. true
    b. false
96. The poet who said that "Life ain't been no crystal stair" was
    a. Langston Hughes
    b. Countee Cullen
    c. James Weldon Johnson
    d. Tupac

97. True or false: some African American artists from Harlem resented the attention they got from whites.

    a. true

    b. false

98. What happens to a dream deferred?

    a. does it dry up like a raisin in the sun?

    b. or fester like a sore and then run?

    c. all of these

    d. Does it stink like rotten meat?

    e. Or crust and sugar over—like a syrupy sweet?

    f. maybe it just sags like a heavy load

    g. Or does it explode?

99. The musical style that became popular during the Harlem Renaissance was

    a. reggae

    b. opera

    c. hip-hop

    d. jazz

100. The Harlem Renaissance author who edited a book of slave folk tales and wrote a novel called <u>Their Eyes Were Watching God</u> was

    a. Langston Hughes

    b. Countee Cullen

    c. Zora Neale Hurston

    d. James Weldon Johnson

101. The branch of philosophy that deals with a person's concept of reality is

    a. metaphysics

    b. epistemology

    c. ethics

    d. politics

102. The branch of philosophy that deals with morality and a person's sense of right and wrong is
   a. metaphysics
   b. epistemology
   c. ethics
   d. politics

103. The branch of philosophy related to government is
   a. metaphysics
   b. epistemology
   c. ethics
   d. politics

104. The branch of philosophy related to the way people know things and find certainty is
   a. metaphysics
   b. epistemology
   c. ethics
   d. politics

105. Ayn Rand's philosophy is called
   a. Objectivism
   b. Realism
   c. Romanticism
   d. Epistomology

106. Ayn Rand was born in
   a. United States
   b. England
   c. France
   d. Russia

107. Ayn Rand believed in this economic system:
   a. communism
   b. socialism
   c. capitalism
   d. bartering

108. Which of the following is not a title of a book by Ayn Rand?

    a. Anthem

    b. Atlas Shrugged

    c. The Fountainhead

    d. A Communist Manifesto

109. True or false? Ayn Rand believed that reality is whatever people shoose for it to be.

    a. true

    b. false

110. True or false? Ayn Rand believed that selfishness is a virtue.

    a. true

    b. false

111. True or false? Ayn Rand was a devout Christian.

    a. true

    b. false

112. True or false? The heroes in Ayn Rand's stories were often weak, meek, and handicapped.

    a. true

    b. false.

113. What pronoun did the citizens in the society of <u>Anthem</u> not use?

    a. They

    b. We

    c. Us

    d. I

114. What was the word that people would be put to death for uttering in that society?

    a. self

    b. community

    c. love

    d. ego

115. What did Equality 7-2521 invent in his tunnel?

    a. fire

    b. the cotton gin

    c. a lightbulb

    d. paper

116. A perfect society is called a
   a. dystopia
   b. utopia
   c. myopia
   d. nudist colony
117. A failed attempt to create a perfect society results in a
   a. dystopia
   b. utopia
   c. myopia
118. One of the themes of <u>Anthem</u> is
   a. the value of teamwork
   b. the triumph of the individual over societal control
   c. the importance of sharing
   d. the blessings that come from serving others
119. During the Enlightenment, authors
   a. celebrated the fulfillment of human potential
   b. cared about knowledge and learning
   c. encouraged creativity and innovation
   d. all of the above
120. The writers of Romanticism
   a. celebrated the imagination and the ideal
   b. used charcters who were every day people in every day
situations
   c. were strict Calvinists
   d. all of the above
121. The writers of Realism
   a. tried to describe life the way it really is
   b. used characters who were every day people in every day
situations
   c. did not use exotic settings
   d. all of the above

122. The literary movement in which writers wrote simple prose and discussed the meaningless of life was
    a. Realism
    b. Romanticism
    c. Puritanism
    d. Modernism
123. The literary movement that Mark Twain was a part of was
    a. Realism
    b. Romanticism
    c. Puritanism
    d. Modernism
124. The two literary movements characterized by a bilief that everything that happens is inevitable and meant to be were
    a. Realism and Romanticism
    b. Naturalism and the Enlightenment
    c. Puritanism and Naturalism
    d. Modernism and the Enlightenment
125. Jonathan Edwards, the writer of "Sinners in the Hands of an Angry God," was a
    a. Puritan
    b. Modernist short story writer
    c. Naturalist
    d. Romantic poet
126. Frederick Douglass was
    a. a slave trader
    b. a farmer and poet
    c. a Harlem Renaissance poet
    d. an abolitionist
127. This writer was from Mississippi:
    a. Flannery O'Connor
    b. Frederick Douglass
    c. William Faulkner
    d. Isaac Asimov

128. This author wrote over 500 books:
   a. Flannery O'Connor
   b. Frederick Douglass
   c. William Faulkner
   d. Isaac Asimov

129. This author wrote <u>The Great Gatsby</u>.
   a. Ernest Hemingway
   b. F. Scott Fitzgerald
   c. Ayn Rand
   d. Isaac Asimov

130. This author taught a chicken how to walk backwards:
   a. Flannery O'Connor
   b. Frederick Douglass
   c. Edgar Allan Poe
   d. F. Scott Fitzgerald

131. This author dropped out of high school:
   a. Flannery O'Connor
   b. Emily Dickinson
   c. William Faulkner
   d. F. Scott Fitzgerald

132. This author taught himself how to read:
   a. William Faulkner
   b. Mark Twain
   c. Isaac Asimov
   d. Frederick Douglass

140. This author had a wife who was mentally ill:
   a. Ernest Hemingway
   b. William Faulkner
   c. F. Scott Fitzgerald
   d. Mark Twain

141. This author married his 13-year-old cousin:
   a. Isaac Asimov
   b. William Falukner
   c. Edgar Allan Poe
   d. Mark Twain

142. This author wrote <u>The Scarlet Letter</u>:
   a. Jonathan Edwards
   b. Emily Dickinson
   c. Edgar Allan Poe
   d. Nathaniel Hawthorne
143. This Harlem Renaissance poet wrote the short story "Thank You Ma'am" about a boy who tries to steal a lady's purse.
   a. Robert Frost
   b. Walt Whitman
   c. Emily Dickinson
   d. Langston Hughes
144. This author lost many of his loved ones to Tuberculosis:
   a. Jonathan Edwards
   b. Mark Twain
   c Edgar Allan Poe
   d. Walt Whitman

Match each vocabulary word to its definition. (definitions deleted)

145. hypocrisy

146. clique

147. persevere

148. antiquated

149. relevant

150. concise

151. blatant

152. morose

153. charisma

154. demeanor

155. bigot

156. legacy

157. glutton

158. hedonism

159. depravity

160. prolific

161. diligence

162. nurture

163. absurd

164. indulgent

Choose the letter of the part of speech of each word in bold.

165. I **have enjoyed** having all of you in my class this year.
   a. noun   b.pronoun   c. verb   d. adverb

166. I wish we could have had a **frog** in our classroom this whole time.
   a. noun   b. pronoun   c. verb   d. adverb

167. I **still** can't believe that our frog died.
   a. noun   b. verb   c. adjective   d. adverb

168. I had a great time reading the entries **in** your journals.

a. adjective   b. conjunction   c. verb   d. preposition

169. If **you** ever need me, look me up on facebook.
   a. noun   b. pronoun   c. conjunction d. verb

170. I hope you will keep reading **and** writing for your whole life.
   a. pronoun   b. adverb   c. conjunction   d. preposition

171. This summer, if you get **bored,** maybe you could read a book for fun.
   a. adverb   b. adjective   c. pronoun   d. noun

172. **Throughout** your college years, you will have to write a lot of papers.
   a. adverb b. conjunction c. preposition d. verb

173. Always cite your sources and **give** credit where it is due.
   a. noun   b. verb   c. adverb   d. pronoun

174. **Never** cheat.
   a. adverb b. pronoun c. noun   d. verb

175. **I** like y'all.
   a. noun   b. pronoun   c. adjective   d. verb

Label each "sentence" as a fragment, a run-on, or "correct."

176. Some of the literature we read was good some was kind of boring.
   a. fragment   b. run-on   c. correct

177. Because the frog died.
   a. fragment   b. run-on   c. correct

178. Some of the literature we read was difficult.

a. fragment   b. run-on   c. correct

179. Don't forget your comma rules, they are important.
a. fragment   b. run-on   c. correct

180. Sometimes you can use semi-colons; they work like periods.
a. fragment   b. run-on   c. correct

181. A comma is not strong enough to connect sentences, it must be followed by a conjunction.
a. fragment   b. run-on   c. correct

182. All sentences must have a subject and a verb.
a. fragment   b. run-on   c. correct

183. Thanks for recycling your plastic bottles I am not that good about recycling.
a. fragment   b. run-on   c. correct

184. without even studying.
a. fragment   b. run-on   c. correct

185. This test is almost over.
a. fragment   b. run-on   c. correct

Label each sentence as simple, compound, or complex.

186. You will study British Literature next year.
a. simple   b. compound   c. complex

187. It might be hard, but y'all are definitely smart enough to handle it.
a. simple   b. compound   c. complex

188. Try to master grammar even though it's not that fun sometimes.
a. simple   b. compound   c. complex

189. I will miss y'all, and I hope you have a good summer.
    a. simple   b. compound   c. complex

190. Americans have written some great literature, and there is a lot of variety.
    a. simple   b. compound   c. complex

191. Though some Americans have written stupid, boring things, others have really written great stuff.
    a. simple   b. compound   c. complex

192. Y'all have written great stuff, too.
    a. simple   b. compound   c. complex

193. I have loved reading your creative writing, and I hope you keep writing poems and stories to share with others.
    a. simple   b. compound   c. complex

194. Why do the lights in my room always flicker on and off?
    a. simple   b. compound   c. complex

195. Maybe there are secret video cameras in the room, and someone turns those lights off whenever I mess up.
    a. simple   b. compound   c. complex

Three of my favorite poems:

The Sun Never Says

by Hafiz (Translated by Daniel Landinsky)

Even after all this time
the sun never says to the earth
"You owe me."
Look what happens with a love like that.
It lights the whole sky.

Those Winter Sundays

by Robert Hayden

Sundays too my father got up early
and put his clothes on in the blueblack cold,
then with cracked hands that ached
from labor in the weekday weather made
banked fires blaze. No one ever thanked him.

I'd wake and hear the cold splintering, breaking.
When the rooms were warm, he'd call,
and slowly I would rise and dress,
fearing the chronic angers of that house,

Speaking indifferently to him,
who had driven out the cold
and polished my good shoes as well.
What did I know, what did I know
of love's austere and lonely offices?

Excerpts from The Raggedy Man
by James Whitcomb Riley

O the Raggedy Man! He works fer Pa;
An' he's the goodest man ever you saw!
He comes to our house every day,
An' waters the horses, an' feeds 'em hay;
An' he opens the shed -- an' we all ist laugh
When he drives out our little old wobble-ly calf;
An' nen -- ef our hired girl says he can --
He milks the cow fer 'Lizabuth Ann.
Ain't he a' awful good Raggedy Man?
Raggedy! Raggedy! Raggedy Man!

An' The Raggedy Man, he knows most rhymes,
An' tells 'em, ef I be good, sometimes:
Knows 'bout Giunts, an' Griffuns, an' Elves,
An' the Squidgicum-Squees 'at swallers the'rselves:
An', wite by the pump in our pasture-lot,
He showed me the hole 'at the Wunks is got,
At lives 'way deep in the ground, an' can
Turn into me, er 'Lizabuth Ann!
Er Ma, er Pa, er The Raggedy Man!
Ain't he a funny old Raggedy Man?
Raggedy! Raggedy! Raggedy Man!

The Raggedy Man -- one time, when he
Wuz makin' a little bow-'n'-orry fer me,
Says "When you're big like your Pa is,
Air you go' to keep a fine store like his--
An' be a rich merchunt -- an' wear fine clothes?
Er what air you go' to be, goodness knows?"
An' nen he laughed at 'Lizabuth Ann,
· An' I says "'M go' to be a Raggedy Man! --
I'm ist go' to be a nice Raggedy Man!"

Raggedy! Raggedy! Raggedy Man!

My People

By Langston Hughes

The night is beautiful,
So the faces of my people.

The stars are beautiful,
So the eyes of my people.

Beautiful, also, is the sun.
Beautiful, also, are the souls of my people.

Say Not The Struggle Not Availeth

By Arthur Hugh Clough

Say not the struggle naught availeth,
The labour and the wounds are vain,
The enemy faints not, nor faileth,
And as things have been they remain.

If hopes were dupes, fears may be liars;
It may be, in yon smoke conceal'd,
Your comrades chase e'en now the fliers,
And, but for you, possess the field.

For while the tired waves, vainly breaking,
Seem here no painful inch to gain,
Far back, through creeks and inlets making,
Comes silent, flooding in, the main.

And not by eastern windows only,
When daylight comes, comes in the light;
In front the sun climbs slow, how slowly!
But westward, look, the land is bright

Refried Bean is from Greenville, SC
Refried worked in a bookstore for twelve years
and has an MFA from Vermont College of Fine Arts.